Communication is the Key

H. Val Peterson

Published By

The Association of Higher Education Facilities Officers

Communication is the Key

Published by:

APPA: The Association of Higher Education Facilities Officers
1643 Prince Street
Alexandria, VA 22314-2818
703-684-1446
www.appa.org

Copyright © 2001 by APPA. All rights reserved.

Printed in the United States of America
International Standard Book Number: 1-890956-16-3

Except as permitted under copyright law, no part of this publication may be reproduced, storied in a retrieval system, distributed, or transmitted, in any form or by any means—electronic, mechanical, photocopying, recording, or otherwise—without the prior written permission of APPA.

Opinions expressed in this book are those of the author and do not necessarily reflect the positions of APPA.

Acknowledgment is made to the following, in which various forms of this book's chapters first appeared:
Facilities Manager · The Image · The Key · Rocky Mountain Views newsletter · Smoke Signals

Editor: Jennifer Graham, APPA
Cover design: Shawn Wilson, Subgraphix
Printing: Digital Graphix

Table of Contents

Preface v

Acknowledgments viii

Section I Communication is the Key

Communication is the Key	3
Please and Thank You	5
Stereotypes Limit Communication	7
Avoid Pompous and Dull Writing	11
Ban Those Rude Phrases	14
The Key	17
What Does Your Image Communicate?	20
If Grounds Could Talk	25
Why in the World Would Anyone Want to Work for a University?	29
The Campus Environment and Learning	32

Section II The Key to Customer Service

Three Cheers for the Students	38
Winning the Service War	41
What Not to Say to Customers	45
Selling the Customer	48
The Customer is King	51
Customer Satisfaction is Job One	54
Handling Customer Complaints	59
That's Not My Job	62
You Are the Department	65
How Good is Your Service?	68

Section III Key Tips for Facilities Professionals

What is a Professional?	72
Moments of Truth	75
Put Your 'Know-How' to Work	79
Personally Inspected By Mary	81
Crafted By K. Minish	83

Criticism	85
Why Integrity Matters	87
Good Intentions	90
Discount Maintenance Is No Bargain	93
Setting and Achieving Goals	97

Section IV   The Key to Leadership and Change

Pursuit of Excellence	102
Staying Focused	106
Chronobiology and You	110
Human Relations	113
Lessons in Leadership	117
Diversity in the Workforce	121
Continuous Improvement and Resistance to Change	124
Change Is Necessary for Progress	129
Technology Demands Change	132
Managing the Campus of the Future	136

Section V   Humor: The Key to Survival

A Message to the Downtrodden	142
It's a Crying Shame	145
How to Get a Raise!	149
Getting No Respect	153
Bad Attitudes	156
Some People are Like Potatoes	160
Needed: A University Garage Sale	163
How to Beat the Meeting Trap	167
Dodging Bullets, Scythes, and Maces	171
The Retirement Report	175

About the Author   183

Preface

In working as a facilities manager for over 33 years one of the most useful principles of organizational management dealt with communication. Customers communicated needs and work requests to our organization. Work orders communicated task and job requirements to supervisors and front-line staff. Reports and tabulated data communicated results to management. And memos, letters, bulletins, and newsletters communicated information to everyone. Effective communication is the lifeblood of every organization.

As a fledgling facilities manager at a major public university, I needed all the help I could get in fulfilling the requirements of the job. My consulting engineering background helped to give me a good technical understanding of buildings and building systems, but it did little else to prepare me for the overall requirements of the job. Good looks and a pleasing personality will only take one so far. My boss did his best to tutor me, but he was anxious to retire after spending 25 years as superintendent of buildings and grounds. His military background had resulted in a somewhat regimented approach to the business of managing facilities.

After about one year on the job, the boss retired, and I was promoted to his job (by then known as director of physical plant), and was left to develop my own mode of operation. As I looked around to see how others approached the job, one of my early role models was Myron "Fife" Fifield, head of plant operations at the University of New Mexico. I had met Fife while attending a Rocky Mountain regional APPA conference. At his institution, Fife published a departmental newsletter named *El*

Servicio Real or "The Royal Service." This newsletter was not the typical, smudgy mimeographed variety, but rather a flashy, slick-finished document with real typesetting and recognizable photographs.

This departmental newsletter was one of several factors gave me an appreciation of two basic principles that have guided me throughout my tenure as a facilities manager. The first principle was professionalism. At a college or university the facilities staff works with professionals in a professional environment, so it is necessary that they perform their services in a professional manner as well.

The second principle was service. The facilities organization exists only to provide service, and I felt strongly that the service provided by my organization ought to be the kind of service that Fife's newsletter promoted - a royal service.

In addition, Fife's newsletter became my inspiration for creating a departmental newsletter at the various universities where I was employed. These newsletters provided an appropriate medium to communicate my ideas, wishes, lessons of life, and philosophy to members of the organization. Sometimes I was accused of "preaching" to the staff through the newsletter. And perhaps that was so. Even though my "preaching" was not along theological lines, my messages gave readers insight into what was important to me and how I felt about a wide variety of issues.

I began writing a regular message in my departmental newsletter that was produced for the sole benefit of my employees. When I changed jobs and started working at another university, it was a natural thing to develop a departmental newsletter for that department too.

Eventually I was appointed editor of a regional newsletter and felt obligated to author an editor's message. After giving up the editor's job, I was asked to hang on as a regular feature writer for the regional newsletter.

Finally, APPA (who published this book) came searching for someone to write a regular feature article on management for its *Facilities Manager* magazine, and I accepted.

I didn't start out my career as an engineer or facilities manager with the thought of becoming a prolific writer, but with time and regularly published articles, I eventually gained that reputation. I would not say that I have a bent for writing, but I do read a fair amount and always maintained a large file of possible ideas for newsletter articles. Sometimes the filed ideas were merely catchy titles. Sometimes it was a bit of useful data or interesting statistics. Other times it dealt with proven practices that could be related to the field of facilities management. Quite often it was just a piece of nonsense that was interesting or funny only to me.

In this book, you will read a sampling of all of the above. Through it all, I have tried to communicate sound principles, proven practices, and helpful ideas. My hope is that I have accomplished that goal. After all, communication is the key.

Acknowledgments

This publication is an anthology of selected articles written for a variety of publications over several decades. These articles come from philosophy dispensed to departmental staff within the facilities management organizations that I directed. Other articles were intended for a much larger readership and were intended to convey management and leadership principles. And yet some articles were an attempt to add a bit of lightness for readers who carried heavy loads and sobering responsibilities.

The publication *El Servicio Real*, the departmental newsletter of the Physical Plant at the University of New Mexico, greatly impressed me as a fledgling facilities manager back in the 1960s. Myron "Fife" Fifield, head of the facilities organization was one of my early role models and his newsletter became my inspiration for creating my own departmental newsletter. I didn't intend to become an author, but article by article the volume grew to be quite extensive.

Thanks is given to the many secretaries and administrative assistants who typed the many articles for the various publications. Time has wiped out the memory of all their names and it would be inappropriate to mention the few that can be remembered. But to all those unnamed individuals, I extend my grateful appreciation.

This book would never have been published except for the persistent encouragement of Fred Giles, an associate at Arizona State University. His ongoing goal of seeing my writings in book form was given life by having all materials collected and retyped. I thank Robin Cook for doing much of the typing and overseeing student typists who worked on the various articles as an ad hoc assignment to their regular duties.

Thanks also go to Steve Glazner, director of communications at APPA, who initiated the original suggestion about publishing an anthology of my writings. I am grateful to Jennifer Graham, publications manager at APPA, for her professionalism in organizing and editing the materials for the book. I thank APPA for taking this step to publish the book.

Though this work has required the assistance of these and other people, the author alone is responsible for its contents.

APPA would also like to thank Betty Farley for compiling edits into the book and assistance with proofreading; and Jason Gray for his editorial assistance.

Section I

Communication is the Key

Communication is the Key

Good communication is essential to the efficient operation of any organization. The lack of good communication with all members of your organization can lead to misinformation, wasted effort, and a feeling of working in the dark.

Sometimes even when we make a special attempt at communication we do not succeed. A note taken from the *Chronicle of Higher Education* highlighted a portion of a memorandum distributed to administrators at an institution of higher education. The memorandum stated in part, "[a]ll offices are now cleaned on a 2/5 system, meaning that they are thoroughly cleaned twice a week and trashed daily."

Now, to a custodian or other facilities professional, the message is perfectly clear. It means that the offices have their carpet vacuumed and furniture dusted twice a week, and the waste baskets are emptied on a daily basis. However, to those unfamiliar with janitor jargon, the term

Communication is the Key

"trashed daily" conjures up visions of a highly vandalized space. This is a benign example of how poor communication or miscommunication can lead to a misunderstanding. But lack of good communication can create situations that are not so easily cleared up.

To communicate there must be a conveying of knowledge or information; it is a process by which information is exchanged. Just because communications fail on occasion, or the fact that it is hard to communicate well, is no excuse for us to avoid the issue. Because of the size and complexity of most facilities management organizations, communication is very important.

One way to improve communications is to publish a regular departmental newsletter. The newsletter can be the media through which the facilities manager can communicate needed information to all employees. The newsletter can be used to communicate a wide variety of messages and information. It can recognize employee accomplishments and successes. It can impart changes in departmental policies and procedures.

The newsletter can bring all areas within a facilities management organization closer together, as the document is able to communicate the purpose and responsibilities of each work unit. It can help people get to know one another better. It can make all employees better informed about what happens throughout the department. Most importantly, it can help make a department feel proud of the accomplishments facilities management makes toward a university or school's mission.

If we are to succeed as a department, subscribe to the truism: Communication is the key.

Please and Thank You

Courtesy refers to considerate behavior toward others, not an outmoded stiff and formal politeness. In its narrowest definition, courtesy includes the use of the words "please" and "thank you" in your day-to-day conversations and communications with others. In its broader sense, courtesy entails issues such as arriving at work on time so that others are not burdened with an extra workload. And in terms of communication, it is a respectful manner in which you express appreciation for another's time and efforts.

Being courteous is an important part of the job for every employee within a facilities management department. First of all, it is certainly more pleasant if your coworkers and your supervisors express courtesies toward one another. Second, most departments have many "customers" in the form of students, staff, faculty, and visitors to campus, and you must communicate with them in a courteous manner. Many times, the image of facilities management and even the institution is determined by how you communi-

Communication is the Key

cate with your customers.

There are many ways in which employees can show consideration for others both inside and outside their facilities department, including:

- arrive to work on time;
- take only allotted time for lunch and breaks;
- limit personal telephone calls;
- leave personal problems at home;
- respect the property of others;
- use leave time ethically;
- avoid destructive gossip;
- avoid terms that are offensive or derogatory to sex, gender, sexual orientation, or ethnic background;
- avoid slang when inappropriate;
- avoid profanity;
- dress in accordance with the institution's image;
- communicate areas of concern before they become major issues;
- take the initiative;
- respect the "chain of command" when expected; and
- provide extra assistance to others when possible.

Take the time to be courteous to everyone around you. Communicate respectfully with others and life will be more enjoyable, especially if you simply say "please" and "thank you" on a regular basis.

Stereotypes Limit Communication

Question: What is white, has wheels, and sleeps four?
Answer: A physical plant van.

If you say the words "maintenance person," some people may form a mental picture in their minds: a person in an oil-spotted work shirt, with buttons straining to hold together fabric stretched tight over a belly, too large to stuff inside a belt, which itself is straining to hold up a massive ring of keys. Some would go so far as to say that a maintenance person is "a necessary evil" or an unpleasant cost of doing business. Where would one find this "maintenance person"? Perhaps in the break room or nowhere to be found.

Within a facilities management organization you'd be hard pressed to find someone who hasn't come face-to-face with these negative perceptions. As with most stereotypes, there may be a grain of truth in these notions, but as the field of maintenance changes, they are far from being accurate or fair.

Communication is the Key

Today, most maintenance organizations include well-trained staff that operate and maintain sophisticated equipment, and work to reduce operating expenses in both maintenance and utility costs. At a college or university with a wide variety of classrooms, laboratories, and equipment, this is doubly so. Typically, facilities employees working in a collegiate environment are exposed to a wider variety of complicated equipment, machinery, and controls. To a great degree, people outside the facilities department have come to recognize the crucial role of maintenance in the overall success of all programs and operations. But still the stereotypes linger.

One of the reasons that these stereotypes continue is the "public face" of maintenance. These are the areas of maintenance most often seen customers, and which often center on the so-called dirty work, such as replacing light bulbs, moving furniture, digging trenches, cleaning toilets, and unclogging sewers. Customers rarely see the more complicated maintenance functions, such as monitoring and adjusting HVAC equipment, operating boilers and chillers in a complex central plant, monitoring and controlling utility usage, generating building plans and drawings from a computer, and using high-tech equipment to produce campus signs. Possibly there are computer controlled irrigation systems, preventive maintenance programs built into campus-wide automation control systems, computer-governed building temperature controls, highly sensitive predictive maintenance techniques, and sophisticated space cleaning equipment. And the list goes on.

Most people have no idea what maintenance people do in a large or small facilities department. They are not around at night to see the response made to an emergency, nor are they on the roof in a downpour to observe the unclogging of a drain, or in a mechanical equipment room where operational adjustments require a real pro. They never see the effort made to restore failed electrical power, or midnight irrigation shifts, or the emergency repairs made to a leaking boiler or chilled water coil, or the scramble necessary to replace a failed compressor.

But let the temperature rise a few degrees, or a waste basket not get emptied, or a light flickering, and there's a crisis to resolve, a letter of explanation to write, and ruffled feathers to smooth. And when the maintenance worker takes a break, everyone assumes he or she is just goofing off.

However, when everything is working, the temperature is within acceptable limits, the buildings are clean, and the grounds are litter free, no one notices. But that is the way of life in maintenance. We are at our best when no one is watching.

In an ideal world, maintenance workers would be judged strictly upon the quality of their work. Maintenance workers themselves can go a long way toward making sure they don't unknowingly communicate the misconceptions that people harbor about them. What can you do? Consider the following:

- Dress and groom like a professional. This doesn't mean sporting a tie to fix a boiler; it just means making sure your clothes are neat and clean.
- Tell others at your organization about maintenance successes.

Communication is the Key

- Keep customer service in mind. Remember that maintenance, like other support services, is customer-driven. Treat your customers as you want to be treated when you are a customer. Better yet, treat your customers as they would want to be treated.

If everyone within an organization works together in a professional manner, communicates facilities activities, and opts to provide quality services at all times, the department and the maintenance workers will receive the appropriate recognition and support that is deserved.

Avoid Pompous and Dull Writing

Facilities professionals should take a firm stand against the use of pompous and stuffy language. This is especially true if it is your own. There are sufficient numbers of pompous and stuffy individuals among the faculty and there is no need to emulate those traits within plant communications. For those of you that have been victims of the messages "please find attached" or "at your earliest convenience," this chapter is for you.

In an organization, written communication comes from two types of people. The first are those who are carried away by their own self-importance and/or insecurity, and they write to impress, not to communicate. Then there are those who are not necessarily important, but they feel they must write in a certain style so as to appear important. In both cases, the writing is terrible. There are the antiquated phrases, the weasel-like ways of saying things, the use of acronyms that are meaningless to all but tenured veterans, the beating around the bush, not getting to the point, and the use of thousand-dollar words, whose meanings can be better stated with a shorter, simpler word.

Communication is the Key

Below are four rules that all communicators should follow, with some bad and good writing examples.

- **Rule: Be conversational.**

Bad: Your earliest attention to the above matter relative to written authorization for local commodities is absolutely imperative.
Good: Please send us your on-campus requisition by Friday.

- **Rule: Avoid jargon.**

Bad: Well-designed documentation is a necessary requisite for an optimized human and machine interface.
Good: If we want people to use the computerized reporting system, we need a manual that's easy to understand.

- **Rule: Avoid antiquated phases.**

Bad: We deem it advisable for you to wait.
Good: We suggest you wait.

- **Rule: Don't depend on acronyms.**

Bad: PROFS Prof Call for IDS of MBA Lab.
Good: Contact Professor Smith by electronic mail for the integrated daytime schedule of the Molecular Biology Absorption Laboratory.

So much for rules. Now for some other tips:

1. Try to keep in mind what's important to the reader, not you. That's how we got in this mess in the first place.
2. If you're doubtful about a sentence, read it aloud to someone else. Be sure to find someone who is brutally honest.
3. Don't try to impress readers with your knowledge. Other than your mother, nobody cares.
4. In a sentence with both good news and bad news, give the bad news first. People generally remember the last thing they're told.
5. If the sentence has double bad news, it's best to avoid that communication.

    Now one last example to bring everything into focus. Keep in mind that to communicate effectively through writing one should decide who the audience is and what is the best form to get a message across.
    There is an often quoted saying that is found in the Bible in Ecclesiastes 9:11:
I turned and saw under the sun, that the race is not to the swift, nor the battle to the strong, neither yet bread to the wise, nor yet riches to men of understanding, nor yet favor to men of skill; but time and chance happeneth to them all.
    See how these words lose their poetry and insightful meaning as they might appear in a government report:
Objective consideration of contemporary phenomena compels the conclusion that success or failure in competitive activities exhibits no tendency to be commensurate with innate capacity, but that a considerable element of the unpredictable must be taken into account.
    Enough said.

Communication is the Key

Ban Those Rude Phrases

Bank tellers in the town of Jinan, a coastal Shandong province in China, are biting their tongues a lot these days. The city's bank recently has banned 90 "uncivilized sentences" and phrases in an attempt to provide "service with a smile."

Some of the forbidden responses include: "I don't know." "That's not my responsibility." "What's the rush?" "Can't you see I'm busy." "Wait over there." "If you don't like it, talk to the management." "Go complain if you want to complain."

The move to ban rude phrases was initiated by the bank's higher-ups to counter the complaint that service in China is notoriously bad. It seems that the idea of the customer being king is an alien concept to employees who deal with the public. Store clerks are too busy chatting with colleagues or reading newspapers to be bothered with helping customers. People who make phone inquiries are routinely hung up on.

As most of us know, bank procedures can be compli

cated and confusing, requiring multiple steps for something as simple as making a deposit or withdrawal. Evidently, tellers in China frequently ignore customers or refuse to look up when customers try to get instructions.

Part of the problem has been attributed to China's communist form of government, which considers service to others as demeaning. The bank considered that a change was necessary since larger numbers of foreigners were demanding better service. These days, customers most everywhere are listened to and the necessary changes were made to meet customer's needs.

As you read this material, did you (as did I) have a slight twinge of guilt in realizing that the situation described can apply to facilities departments? Can you think of certain employees who exhibit these attitudes outside the banking world and a lot closer to home than China? Elements of these attitudes exist to some degree or another in most organizations and, yes, even within facilities management operations.

Who has not heard or received a complaint about some of the following phrases? Or, heaven forbid, have you possibly used some of these yourself?

"Fill out a work order request form and we will take care of it." "Our budget doesn't cover that sort of thing." "What's the beef, the cost seems reasonable to me." "Our policy doesn't allow us to do that." "We've always done it that way." "The person in charge is not here today." "We will get to it next week or the week after for sure." "Due to budget cuts, we no longer provide that service."

Let's face it, customers (students, faculty, academic staff, and others) are demanding better service—both away

Communication is the Key

from work and on the job. I fear that sometimes as service providers we take our customers for granted. In a facilities organization, individuals sometimes assume that one can work in relative anonymity because they are part of a larger organization. One can rationalize that the significance of his or her work will never be noticed. But it does get noticed! Your individual behavior communicates a message about you and the entire organization that you represent.

In the business world, satisfying customers is the secret of success. Believe it or not, it is also the secret of success for a good facilities organization. This also means that it's the secret for individual success, whether this is the campus or organization community in general or a particular building or area where you are assigned to work. Only when each employee commits to provide customer-oriented service and follows through in that commitment, does a facilities department give customers their "money's worth."

Each facilities organization would do well to analyze its customer service practices to pinpoint any "uncivilized sentences" or phrases that should be banned. Customer service starts with courteous communication and the right attitude, exhibited by customer-friendly responses.

The Key

The *Key* seems an odd name for a newsletter. Why would a facilities management department name it's newsletter *The Key*?

When I headed the facilities department at Arizona State University, I named our newsletter *The Key* for a number of reasons. I would like to share them as the reasons are universal and can apply to any facilities department regardless of whether you have a newsletter or not.

The facilities management department is the keystone of an educational organization. Among other definitions for "key", Webster's Dictionary lists the following:

- "of basic importance"
- "something that gives an explanation or identification or provides a solution"
- "a keystone in an arch"

Typically, the facilities management organization is one of basic importance to the institution it serves.

Communication is the Key

Employees within this organization are regularly called upon to give explanations, make identifications, and provide solutions to everyday needs of the campus. While we recognize that academic programs and research functions are key to the institution, facilities management acts as the keystone of the total organization. Without the vital functions and services performed by facilities management, everything would tend to fall apart, just as the arch falls down without the keystone.

The key to college or university success is facilities management. In many ways, the facilities management organization is key to the successful operation of the institution it serves. The services provided by facilities management allow the various operations of the institution to take place. This unit fixes things when they break and replaces them when they are deemed "unfixable." It insures that electrical power is available for lights, equipment operations, and air conditioning. It makes sure the restrooms and drinking fountains are functioning. It operates a central plant that provides essential utility services on a continuous basis. It fixes the roofs when they leak. It repaints the walls when needed. It makes sure the doors will lock. It fixes broken cabinets. It disposes of tons of litter and garbage generated each day on campus. It makes the place look nice. It makes it comfortable. Without these essential services, most other operations of the institution would grind to a halt.

People are the key. The key ingredient in a successful facilities management organization is good people. Employees in the facilities management unit are like the carbonation in cool and refreshing soft drinks. When they

Communication is the Key

are good, they add zest, sparkle, and essence to the organization just as the carbonation does to the drink. Without good people the organization is flat, without life, and unpalatable-not unlike the soft drink that has lost its fizz.

Good people are those who try to do their jobs each day and perhaps even a bit more. Good people make a worthwhile contribution to their crew or shop. Good people want to learn, grow, and progress. Good people look for better and more efficient ways to accomplish their assigned tasks. Good people are helpful, friendly, tolerant, and courteous to others. Good people know what needs to be done and do it. Good people that are dedicated and hard working are the sum and total of what facilities management should be about.

Good people are the key to success. And each employee is the key.

What Does Your Image Communicate?

One definition of image is, "a mental conception held in common by members of a group and symbolic of a basic attitude or orientation." This definition seems a bit academic to me so I made-up my own: "image is how you or it are seen by others." In some vocations or professions, image is highly critical. In some businesses and corporations, image means survival or failure. In some educational institutions, image is carefully crafted and managed.

Let's bring the concept of image closer to home. What is your own personal image? What is the image of your facilities organization? What image does your organization communicate based upon the condition and appearance of its grounds and buildings, or other facilities?

For those of us who work within a facilities department, these three images are certainly interrelated and are worthy of our close attention.

Individual Image. The image of any organization is a direct reflection of its employees. From the standpoint of your customers, the facilities department image is you. Every employee in the organization contributes to the overall image of the department. A positive personal image is created by communicating in a friendly demeanor and a firm voice, by standing tall and walking proudly, by eye contact and a firm handshake, and by maintaining honesty and integrity.

People tend to look at little things in developing their first impression about individuals. In the long run, however, people may doubt what individuals say, but they believe what they do. It's the old adage that, actions speak louder than words. Communication is not limited to verbal expression, but includes physical expression and outside demeanor. The right image fosters not only a positive reaction from customers but creates greater employee self-esteem and productivity. Every facilities department has scores of competent, hard-working, and dedicated employees. Without the efforts of its employees, the facilities department is nothing.

Without people there can be no image, only an empty reflection. What is your personal image. Are you viewed as being responsible and professional and responsive? Are you a competent and consistent communicator? Are you firm but fair? For some, your organization will be judged by the image you personally present to the customer.

Departmental Image. It should be assumed that facilities professionals want their departments to have a good image. Most are anxiously engaged in the continual improvement of this image. To this end, it is important for the various customers to know of facilities-related happenings around them that could affect their own jobs or organizations. It's always a good idea to share the accomplishments, the good works, and the recognition of individual teams and work units within the facilities group. These types of communications can best be done through a departmental newsletter, a bulletin distributed to a broad cross section of the organization, articles published in the organization's newsletter or other publications, and one-on-one meetings and conversations with customers. These actions all support the creation and preservation of a favorable image.

Positive efforts of the department, however, can be negated if some of the lesser details are not handled properly. It might be well to ask yourself the following questions:

- How are your phones being answered? Do employees give their names when answering, so that callers feel that they're dealing with a real person instead of an institution?

- How are visitors greeted when they visit the department? Are they acknowledged promptly, or are they made to wait until someone gets good and ready to approach them? If the receptionist is on the phone, does he or she tell the visitor, "I'll be with you in a moment?"

- When greeting visitors or customers, do your employees convey positive body language? Do they smile? Studies show that the most important thing in communicating a favorable impression is how often you smile.

- Is someone responsible for ensuring that all communications don't go out with misspellings or grammatical errors? Someone once said, "You are what you mail."

- Do requests for service get acknowledged? Is a date given the customer when the service will take place? If there was a delay, was it communicated? If it is not obvious that the service has been completed, is the customer informed that the work has been done? Is there follow-up at the end of the job to make sure the service was satisfactory? These are common courtesies extended to customers in the private sector. If we are not doing these things, we may be inviting the privatization of our own organizations.

Your answers to these questions (and many more) are indicators of how customer service is viewed within your organization. Good service is expected-and needed. And good service equates to a positive image.

Institutional Image. We are all aware of the Carnegie Foundation study that confirmed the feeling of most facilities professionals that the work performed by the facilities department has a direct bearing upon the image of the college or university. Students and parents look at the condition of the buildings and grounds when selecting an institution for matriculation. Have you looked closely at your buildings and grounds recently? Do the buildings show excessive signs of wear and tear? Do the lawns look shaggy and the shrubbery neglected? Are the sidewalks broken and cracked? Are campus signs hard to understand and in poor repair? If so, that gives a negative image of the institution.

The physical presence of the campus tends to serve as the "entrance gate" for critical spectators and influential constituencies from which an initial impression is generated and an image firmly entrenched. It is from this group that the institution hopes to attract students, faculty, and staff as well as philanthropic contributions, gifts, and endowments. A well managed and maintained physical environment offers an inviting welcome sign for all to see and enjoy. It is important to understand that looks do matter, and that first impressions in particular matter a great deal.

Institutions, like people, are judged by their appearance. If the appearance is neat, clean, and attractive, then the judgment is positive. If, on the other hand, the appearance is shabby, dirty and unkempt, the judgment will be negative.

There is an old truism that goes something like, "You only get one chance to make a first impression." This saying applies to individuals, to organizations, and to institutions. Images are developed from first impressions. It may take months and even years to change an image formed in a few short seconds as a first impression.

All people, organizations, and institutions have an image. What does your image communicate about you?

If Grounds Could Talk

Have you ever stopped to think about the importance of your campus landscape? Is it just grass to mow, leaves to rake, and weeds to pull? If so, why bother?

More and more people are realizing the value of landscapes, but do not necessarily realize why. Landscapes are important because plants arranged in a harmonious and attractive manner make a major contribution toward enhancing the quality of our lives. A variety of scientific research projects conducted by psychologists, geographers, architects, horticulturists, and landscape architects have measured the impact that plants and landscapes make in our day-to-day lives, and that impact is significant.

In the public sector, landscaping is important from two standpoints. First, attractive landscaping provides a great showplace for potential investors in other properties. Investors seem to be intrigued by intensive and attractive landscaping because it enhances the overall image of the property. Second, landscaping is just good business. Many businesses and developments use landscaping to attract customers. I once visited the Pier 39 development in San Francisco and was impressed how landscaping was used as a feature to attract customers. They even have specific events that focus on the landscaping, such as Tulipmania which showcases more than 15,000 multi-colored tulips each spring.

Just as landscaping plays a big part in attracting and retaining good tenants and customers in the business world, the influence of the landscape has also proven to be a very important part of marketing and promotion for many colleges, universities, and schools.

In the mid-1980s, the Carnegie Foundation for the Advancement of Teaching published the results of a study evaluating the college experience in America. The study found that the campus appearance (buildings, trees, well-maintained lawns and walkways) was the most influential factor related to a high school senior's decision of what college to attend. It can be reasonably extrapolated that an attractively landscaped setting also contributes to attracting and retaining staff and faculty as well.

Impressions, attitudes, and decisions are shaped by the visual condition of a campus. Typically, the landscape is the first thing people see when visiting a school and the landscape can determine enrollment or employment. It can also enhance the possibility of gifts and donations to the institution. Because the grounds can be one of the best recruiting tools available to the campus, ground development and care should not be neglected. A campus may well derive its distinction through the fine balance between aesthetically pleasing buildings and a carefully landscaped environment.

Ernest L. Boyer, author of *College: The Undergraduate Experience in America*, said, after reviewing a large number of college brochures, "… it would be easy to conclude that about one-half of all college classes are held outside, on a sunny day by a tree, close to water…." It is obvious that the landscape is an excellent marketing tool, but it also has significant value as an employee benefit. With this in mind, landscaping must be viewed as much more than just filler that connects together campus buildings.

Most educators will agree that well-maintained buildings and grounds are essential for a proper learning environment. Research conducted in this area indicates that student achievement test scores are higher where the learning environment is well maintained and attractive. Cosmetic factors were found to be more important then functional factors, and student performance was even found to be better in classrooms with windows. So academic performance suffers when the inside and outside environments are neglected.

What does this all mean for the facilities professional? It means that the landscapes you create are not just an amenity, but an essential marketing and retention tool. It means that the landscape is an asset with value even greater than its monetary worth to your organization. It means that the landscape manager's job continues to become more important and highly respected. Looking at the big picture, one comes to the realization that the actual value of the landscape on a college and university or school campus escalates the need for expertise, professionalism, and commitment to campus landscape management.

Finally, it means that you shouldn't underestimate what the grounds communicate about you and your organization.

Communication is the Key

Why in the World Would Anyone Want to Work for a University?

Working at a college or university is not easy. Over the years budget reductions have become a way of life. There have been layoffs and years when no raises were given to staff. Unit operating budgets have been reduced to the point that needed supplies, materials, and equipment have been in short supply. One might well ask themselves, "Why in the world would anyone want to work for a university?"

Even though arguments can be made for how bad things have been in the past, it is always instructive to look at the other side of the coin to see what is good. There are numerous reasons why a university is found to be a good place to work and these reasons may be highlighted in an employee survey conducted within your facilities management department. Numerous studies have uncovered some of the most common reasons given for employee job satisfaction.

Help from coworkers. There is a cooperative spirit

within facilities management organizations of mutual cooperation between individuals within the same and different work units. This statement can be heard over and over again, "I like the good people I work with."

Favorable work environment. The work environment at a university is a real plus. On the whole it is clean, safe, and well maintained. The buildings are pleasant and the grounds attractive. The quality of life that surrounds staff is one to be enjoyed and appreciated. For the people that work at a university, or those who come and go, the emphasis is the same—to improve and expand knowledge.

Involvement in a worthwhile endeavor. A university is involved not only in the development of young people to be productive and contributing members of society, but it makes great contributions to the discovery of new knowledge through research and by giving public service in a variety of ways. Few places of employment make such a significant contribution to society.

Comprehensive benefits package. While most employers offer benefits, employees at a university typically enjoy fringe benefits that are envied by individuals working elsewhere. Not only do university employees enjoy liberal vacation, sick leave, and other types of special leave benefits, but also the group medical and dental insurance benefits are essential given today's high health care costs. Perhaps one of the most rewarding benefits is allowing each employee, as well as spouses and children, to enjoy the value of an education at a greatly reduced cost.

Ever changing environment. A university is a dynamic entity that is ever growing and changing. Unlike those people who spend their lives doing routine, assembly line tasks, most employees never know from day to day what their exact tasks may be. This makes the job more enjoyable.

There are other good reasons why the university is a good place to work, but the above items are the most often noted by employees. Life is much more enjoyable if we dwell on the good rather than the bad. The bad in life will always be with us but then so will the good. We should not let our fears about the bad things that may happen in the future control our present thoughts and actions. What matters is that we not allow our fears to produce a mental paralysis so that we only do enough to make it through each day.

I appreciated working for a university. While there are always circumstances that could be better, it is still a great place to work. Sometimes one feels that the grass is greener on the other side of the fence, but usually when you cross the fence and look back from where you came, the grass is greener there too. Be appreciative of what you have and give your best to the organization you work for.

The Campus Environment and Learning

Almost every educator will agree that a well-maintained teaching facility is essential for a proper learning environment. Yet no one has been able to prove that the quality of a facility directly affects student learning concretely or scientifically.

A struggle for facilities professionals is emphasizing the relationship that educators intuitively seem to understand-that the condition of facilities is an important element in the overall learning process. Many of us may recall the study conducted in the mid-1980s by the Carnegie Foundation for the Advancement of Teaching wherein the condition of the buildings and grounds was identified as a major factor influencing the student's choice of a particular institution to attend. Nothing in the study, however, tied the condition of facilities and grounds to successful learning.

A more recent article published in *Business Officer* magazine noted that "a campus's physical presence typically serves as the 'front door' for key audiences and important constituencies, creating an initial—and often enduring—image within the community from which it hopes to attract students, faculty, and staff." As competition intensifies for the best and brightest students, faculty, and staff, the physical amenities figure more prominently in the decision-making process. Prospective students and their parents compare dormitories. Professors in high demand look closely at libraries and research facilities.

The *Wall Street Journal* carried an article about an Ivy League sophomore, who originally intended to enroll at one university, but changed her mind when a campus visit to another school convinced her that their campus amenities were much better.

For those of us who have attended schools in the past or attended meetings, workshops, and seminars where the building environment and its maintenance were both lacking, can probably recall examples of distractions created by noisy pipes, uncomfortable temperatures, peeling paint, objectionable odors, broken window blinds, flickering lights, and a host of other annoying conditions. When any of the human senses of sight, hearing, smell, taste, or touch are disturbed by unusual or distracting stimuli, mental concentration is interrupted and the mind tends to focus on the distractions rather than what is being said or presented. These distractions can be as disturbing to the teacher as they are to the student.

Not only can the condition of the facility be distracting but it can also create an "I don't care" attitude as well. In "I don't care" surroundings, human attitudes deteriorate at an even greater rate.

While there is no absolute proof linking the condition of the building environment and successful student learning within that environment, there have been attempts made to make this connection. The difficulty seems to lie in being able to isolate the variables that influence student behavior. The process presents some major problems of methodology and makes any research effort in this area somewhat tenuous.

The results of some studies in elementary and secondary schools that evaluated the possible relationship between selected student variables and the condition of the school buildings, which the student attended, was reported in the January 1997 issue of *School Planning & Management* magazine. The studies found a positive relationship between building condition and student academic performance. In all the studies, student achievement test scores were higher in well-maintained buildings. The greatest increases were found more often in cosmetic factors such as paint, cleanliness, furniture, graffiti control, and grounds.

Several specific building conditions had a positive effect on performance. For example, student test scores were higher in buildings that had windows in the classroom, less graffiti, better locker conditions and acoustical ceilings. In one study higher scores occurred in building with air conditioning and recently painted exterior walls.

Based on the research in this area, there was no doubt that building condition affects academic performance. The only remaining issue is whether the educational benefit outweighs the financial cost. A new building may not be necessary, but attention to air conditioning, furniture repair, building maintenance, graffiti removal, and general cleanliness are all important aspects of the learning process. Even though the aforementioned studies were not conducted at colleges and universities, the same results might be anticipated at institutions of higher education.

    If teachers and professors are to succeed in enhancing the learning environment at their institutions, they must use every means possible to convince decision-makers that the condition of the facilities has a direct relationship to the success of student learning. The point needs to be driven home that recent research supports the case that academic performance suffers when building condition is neglected. Let the lobbying begin (or continue)!

Section II

The Key to Customer Service

Three Cheers for the Students

Attracting and retaining students is a major concern at most colleges and universities. Institutions recruit students from all around the world offering scholarships and other incentives. Once students arrive on the campus, numerous programs are geared to mentor them and to keep them satisfied while enrolled at the institution.

Sometimes campus administrators remind employees about the importance of the role they play as they interact with students on an ongoing basis. Facilities professionals also have the opportunity to remind their staff about the important role they play in the area of attracting and retaining students. The facilities staff can ensure that students will be satisfied while on campus by treating them with courtesy and respect and making a concerted and consistent effort to meet their needs.

While association with students by facilities staff may be somewhat limited and indirect, it does make a difference in the student's attitude about the institution if the staff treats them as if they are pleased to be of service

The Key to Customer Service

whenever the opportunity arises. Positive contacts and relationships with all faculty and staff members is a major factor that influences students to continue their studies at the institution.

Here are some suggestions for consideration by facilities management staff that will help to maintain a proper perspective toward students:

1. Students are the most important individuals on campus. Without students there would be no need for the institution or its employees.
2. Students are not cold enrollment statistics but flesh and blood human beings with feelings and emotions.
3. Students are not just people to be tolerated so that you can do your own thing. They are your thing.
4. Students are not dependent upon you. Rather, you are dependent on them.
5. Students are not an interruption of your work, but rather the purpose of it.
6. You are not doing the students a favor by serving them. They are doing you a favor by giving you the opportunity to do so.

If you keep these six factors in mind as you go about your daily activities and jobs, it will help you maintain an appropriate attitude toward students.

For those of you who have had the experience of being a college student, you know that the life of a student is often filled with frustration, discouragement, worries, and financial problems. The life of a student is not an easy one. If the facilities management organization can offer an

Communication is the Key

extra degree of courtesy, helpfulness, and friendliness to the students, it just might make their lives a little more enjoyable—or at least tolerable. A kindness shown by a single employee might just be the reason a person doesn't drop out of school.

And it just might make the difference about their attitude toward the institution in determining whether or not they continue as students. We need the students.

Winning the Service War

An article in *Management Review* magazine entitled "Five Ways to Win the Service War," by John Humble, stated that "Service is not a management trend that is going to die in one or two years. In today's economic climate, it's often what separates business survivors from casualties. Accordingly, senior management executives of 615 companies put 'service quality' at the top of their lists when asked by the Gallup Organization to prioritize eight business concerns."

It is clear that this article was written for the private sector, but within our own service organizations there are lessons to be learned. It is a fact the world over that as competition has intensified, quality and service to customers are issues that have come to the forefront. In most areas, the principles involved are as applicable to the educational facilities manager as for managers of manufacturing companies and private service organizations. We need to pay attention before some form of organizational Armageddon strikes.

Communication is the Key

In the business world, key types and groups of customers are targeted for satisfaction. No facilities management organization can afford to satisfy all its "customers," which typically includes all students, staff, faculty, and administration. But there are key areas to be satisfied, and so attention should be focused on a selected group. In most instances, the deans are a good place to start, and selected department heads are a good choice too. The result is to listen carefully and be responsive to the perceived needs. Efforts spent in this area will be well repaid and may be the most essential thing you can do. When facilities managers take time to listen to their "customers" they may be surprised to find how often quality and service rank higher than lowest cost.

Another lesson to be learned from the private sector is that satisfied customers are loyal. It never hurts to keep the campus community apprised of new technology and application within the department. Distributing your department's newsletter, and sponsoring seminars to keep them abreast of important changes and areas of interface, are only two examples of the efforts that can build strong and lasting relationships.

Measuring customer satisfaction is yet another technique used in the business world that can be of benefit if you are really interested in having a first-class facilities management organization. Many times recipients of poor service never bother to complain to the department, but they continually badmouth the organization to all whom will listen. Negative customer experiences, whether experienced or overheard, all add up to a bad image for the provider of the service. Therefore, a monthly survey, for example, can give you feedback about your customer service efforts.

In the private sector, successful businesses try to know their enemy. It is extremely discouraging on occasion to find out that "the enemy is us." The facilities manager needs to know the type and quality of service being rendered by the staff. The manager needs to get out of his or her office and look at the quality and timeliness of maintenance, chargeback, and capital improvements. Does it measure up in quality? Was it performed on a timely basis? Were the charges reasonable? Sometimes it is enlightening to call your service center or other operations that interface regularly with the campus to find out if they respond courteously; if they are helpful, efficient, and accurate. Ask yourself based upon this telephone contact whether or not you would be a satisfied customer.

Good facilities managers know that the whole is greater than the sum of its parts. Starting with the needs of the students and faculty, managers must set overall quality and performance goals, associated with levels of courtesy and problem solving, for all employees. Consider this quote from the book *Service America* by Ron Zemke and Karl Albrecht, "Our hospital is organized and managed by professional specialty—by functions like nursing, housekeeping, security, pharmacy, and so on. As a result, no single person or group is really accountable for the overall success and quality of the patients' experience." Think about it.

In the end, good service is all about the people in your organization. Research in the private sector has found that when employees view an organization's human resources policies favorably, customers view the quality of service they receive favorably. Selecting the right people, training them well and imaginatively, counseling and motivating them are not options but imperatives for today's facilities manager. The image of your organization is most often in the hands of the workers who interact with customers. That's why the Disneyland theme parks train their ticket collectors for four full days. The way the customer is treated is one of the most powerful ways to shape their perception of the organization and its quality.

Take time to step back and take a look at your organization from the customer's point of view. If you like what you see, great! If not, you might want to borrow some techniques from the private sector to help make improvements.

The Key to Customer Service

What Not to Say to Customers

I would have to say that the field of facilities management has made good progress over the past several years in being customer service oriented. A critical element of customer service is how each employee interacts with customers during one-on-one encounters. What you say and how you say it can add to or detract from the customer's opinion of our service orientation. There are at least five forbidden phrases that should be banned from your on-the-job vocabulary. The following paragraphs focus on these phrases, as they relate to customer service, and suggestions for what to say instead.

"No!"

Remember how deflated and even angry you felt as a child when an urgent request to your parents was met with this response? This one word denotes total rejection. Erase it from your memory as a customer response word. Alternative responses should stress the positives of what can be done, for example: "We aren't able to refund your account, but we can replace the faulty work at no additional charge."

"Hang on a second, I'll be right back."
First of all, it will take longer than a second to find the item needed or the answer to a question, so you won't be right back. A better approach is: "I'll be glad to find that information for you, but it will take a couple of minutes. Would you like to wait or shall I contact you after I have the answer?" Customers left standing at the counter or hanging on the telephone appreciate an honest assessment of the time required to answer their inquiry.

"I don't know."
If you honestly don't know then you should find out. An alternate response would be: "That's a good question. I'd be happy to find the answer for you. I will get back to you just as soon as I have the information." The I-don't-know response usually carries the additional message "I don't care" in the minds of your customers.

"We can't do that."
Imagine your reaction if you heard this comment as a customer. Your defenses would go up and you would dig in your heels for a fight. Instead, try something like this: "That's a tough one. Let me see what I can do." Or you could say, with a positive spin, "I see why you are asking for that. Here's what I can do to solve the problem."

"You'll have to…"
Once again, these words leave the customer feeling as if

there are no options. To say nothing of feeling defensive by being told what to do. Try responding in this way: "Here's what you can do…" or "Here's how we can help you with that." Taking some responsibility in helping the customers resolve an issue or getting the information needed raises your level of service considerably in the eye of the customer.

    While these suggested scenarios won't eliminate all misunderstandings, they can go a long way to reduce many of the daily hassles that arise as you deal with your customers.

Communication is the Key

Selling the Customer

Joe Girard is listed in the Guinness Book of World Records as the world's greatest salesperson. Joe says that customers "don't buy Chevrolets, they buy me."

In today's marketplace people making major purchases must "buy" the person selling the product before they'll purchase the product. In other words, salespeople must sell themselves to their customers.

While we in facilities management do not sell a product, we do provide a service and in many cases we literally "sell" this service to our customers as chargeback work. Irrespective of whether customers pay for our services, we must in essence sell ourselves as individuals in order to earn their respect, confidence, and approval for the services provided. Here's how to be successful in this area.

Be the customer's consultant. Many customers have a vague idea of what they want, but need guidance in getting the desired result. In this instance we must provide professional assistance to guide their decisions. We must function as a consultant. The key to successful consulting is fact-finding. Ask questions, listen, and survey for information as needed.

Have a high level of enthusiasm. Experts in all areas agree that at least half of the successes in business, art, science, or politics can be attributed to enthusiasm. In fact, Ralph Waldo Emerson said, "Nothing great was ever achieved without enthusiasm." As an employee of a facilities management organization you must be sold on your own organization and its ability to meet customer's needs. People who are enthusiastic about making customer's lives better are those who are most successful.

Be extraordinarily organized. Humans are drawn to order. The more organized you are, the more you are trusted. You don't need to tell people you are organized, they will know. Be on time. Have everything you need with you. Never "wing it" on a service visit. Assume that the customer's time is much too valuable for that and always plan ahead to be prepared.

Build a bond. Most of us would rather do business with people like us. No matter what your background or job, you can always find things in common with the customer. Be friendly, sincere, and comment on shared interests. Dale Carnegie said, "You can make more friends in two months by becoming interested in other people than you can in two years by trying to get other people interested in you."

Focus on the customer. In the marketplace you buy from people who show interest in your needs. Our customers not only want service, but they want to know you care. It has been said that people don't care how much you know until they know how much you care. Start with little things, such as using the customer's name (pronounced correctly, of course). Take notes of what they say or want. Working from the customer's point of view helps you and the customer to become a problem-solving team. Take full responsibility to solve their problem or meet their needs.

Prove your expertise. Expertise is proven by actions, not words. Emerson said, "What you do speaks so loudly, I cannot hear what you say." Don't tell them how good you are, show them. Be ready to prove your expertise. Experts are confident, even when facing a problem for the first time. You don't need to be an authority in all areas, but you must be able to discover problems and unrecognized needs in order to provide good solutions.

Build trust. Experts in human behavior maintain that the mental impression you make in the first two seconds is so striking that it takes another four minutes to add 50 percent more to the impression. Before you reach out your hand or open your mouth, your customer's mind is processing years of imbedded perceptions to determine if you can be trusted. Make sure your first impression says this person can be trusted. Trust is absolute confidence in the honesty, reliability, and integrity of another person. Trust is hard to gain, easy to loose, and critical to your success.

Facilities management employees who follow these suggestions will not only find that their relationships with customers will be at the highest levels, but they will also find more satisfaction in their jobs.

The Key to Customer Service

The Customer is King

All of us have heard the saying, "the customer is king," but we usually think that the saying only applies to retail sales. No mater what product a company produces or services it provides, the company couldn't exist without customers. Your institution has its customers. They are the students, and also to a lesser degree, the student's families, as well as the faculty and staff.

Sometimes, you take your customers for granted as human beings. You assume you can work in relative anonymity because you are part of an organization. You may rationalize that the significance of your work will be unnoticed.

Satisfying customers is not only the secret of success in business, but in a good facilities management operation as well. This also means that the secret of your individual success is how well you satisfy customers—whether this be the campus community in general or only those people in the particular building or area where you are assigned to

Communication is the Key

work. Only when you and your coworkers provide good service do you give your customers their money's worth.

Your everyday work affects customers regardless of whether or not you deal directly with them. An incorrect delivery, a carelessly installed product, a mistake in billing, a room that is continually too hot or too cold are all noticed by customers.

Careless or shoddy work can sometimes result in much bigger problems. As a case in point, take this chain of events, which happened at a pump company. A rush order for pumps and auxiliary equipment was shipped by truck from the company's plant to a construction site in a neighboring state. Before the equipment left, a shipping clerk put the installation drawings in a heavy plastic envelope attached to the side of one of eight crates. When the shipment arrived at its destination, the crates were stored outdoors. No one took the plans out of the envelope, and although a yardman was told to cover the crates with a plastic tarp, he didn't. It rained hard overnight, ruining the plans. The plastic zipper at the top had not been tightly sealed, allowing the envelope to fill with water.

Whose fault was it? The shipping clerk at the pump company denied he had forgotten to close the zipper; the receiving clerk said he didn't remove the plans from the envelope because "it wasn't my responsibility"; and the yardman couldn't be found the next day.

This story is an example of an unfortunate sequence of errors and oversights. The result was a costly delay in the installation of urgently needed equipment and a very dissatisfied customer. All of the problems could have easily been avoided if each person involved had just kept in mind

The Key to Customer Service

that the customer was anxiously waiting for this equipment to be properly installed.

If it occasionally irritates you that your supervisor insists upon more careful work, speedier deliveries, better service, and so on, keep in mind that it's really your customers who insist upon these things.

Within your organization, it's part of everyone's job to satisfy the customer. You usually don't get much feedback from customers unless they're unhappy. But when you don't hear from them, you want to feel confident that it's because they are happy. After all, if the customers are happy it means you are doing your job.

Customer Satisfaction is Job One

The decade of the 1990s marked the 100th anniversary of the American automobile industry. Historians have credited the Duryea brothers of Springfield, Massachusetts for the start of this industry in America. In 1896, the brothers J. Frank and Charles produced 13 cars from the same design. A 4-horsepower, 1-cylinder engine powered the car. Although the very first American car was built back in 1805, this was the first time that more than one vehicle was produced from the same design. Prior efforts had been to produce one-of-a-kind and start-from-scratch type vehicles.

Ford Motor Company entered the business world without fanfare in 1903. This pioneering company founded by Henry Ford was to become one of the world's largest corporations. Few companies are as closely identified with the history and development of America throughout the 20th century as Ford. And perhaps no other American firm is as well known around the world.

At the time of its founding, Ford was a tiny operation doing business out of a converted Detroit wagon factory staffed with about ten people. In the first 15 months of operation, 1,700 Model A passenger cars were cranked out of the old wagon factory. Records show that by 1908, 485 different companies were building the horseless carriages, but the most successful of all these vehicles was the Ford Model T. The first Model T was delivered October 1, 1908, and Ford Motor Company has been mass-producing cars ever since. Henry Ford is credited with putting America on wheels, by producing a car within the means of the working class. Today, the company is the world's second-largest producer of cars and trucks, with manufacturing, assembly, or sales operations in 30 countries, on six continents.

A number of year's back, in an attempt to offset criticism about the inferior quality of their vehicles as compared to those manufactured in other countries, Ford adopted the motto quality is job one. This theme was intended to inspire workers to perform quality work and to assure customers that the design and workmanship of Ford-produced products was guaranteed to be of the highest quality. One of Ford's most successful car dealerships took this same concept a bit further by saying that within their particular dealership customer service is "job one." This highly focused attention on customer satisfaction led them to achieve phenomenal success in sales and service.

Though facilities management organizations do not sell automobiles, the wisdom expressed by that one Ford dealership can benefit us as we serve our own customers. We might do well to consider how these five rules, promoted by the Ford dealership, could apply to facilities operations.

Communication is the Key

Rule 1: Never tell a customer that a problem can't be fixed. When a customer has a problem, the last thing they want to hear is "that's the way it is, live with it." It is important to listen to the customer to identify the problem and then make an honest attempt to have it resolved. Some problems are easier to resolve than others are, and sometimes the resolution to the problem is not always obvious. Don't drop the problem after making the first pass at fixing it. If repeated attempts are necessary, make sure you are working on the right problem. If the "fix" requires an extended period of time, keep the customer informed.

Rule 2: Never promise too much, and always do a little more than you promised to do. Taking responsibility to look into a customer's request is expected, but caution must be used in promising something that can't be delivered. Make sure you fully understand the issue before making any promises. No one wins when false expectations are created. Know the limits of what can be accomplished and the time frame within which it can be scheduled and completed. On the other hand, one builds credibility with the customers by doing more than what they ask for. Sometimes that may be no more than completing a project ahead of schedule or doing it for less cost than was originally estimated.

Rule 3: Treat your customer's needs first. In the private sector, organizations that are most successful depend upon having customers come back again. Dissatisfied customers usually react first by using their mouth to complain, and then secondly they use their feet to walk down the street to do business with a competitor. In our case, we need to make it a priority in meeting customer's needs so that our organization minimizes complaints and criticism, as well as minimizing the need to consider privatization options. Always remember that if it weren't for the purpose of meeting your customer's needs, your organization would not be necessary at all.

Rule 4: Give all customers a fair deal. Some customers are more demanding than others. But it's not good to give preferential treatment or better service to one customer and then try to make it up on another. All customers should be treated with consistency and fairness. Don't fall into the trap of dropping everything else to "grease the squeaking wheel." While attending to the problems of the "wheel," other less vocal customers may be experiencing a slow burn from neglect.

Rule 5: Fix the problem the first time you handle it. It is highly frustrating to a customer to repeatedly request that the same concern or problem is addressed. In addition, it is highly inefficient an employee to make multiple attempts to resolve the same issue. The organization that makes repeated unsuccessful attempts to fix the same problem loses credibility and the customer is left with a lack of confidence in the organization's ability to resolve problems.

Just as Ford Motor Company has promoted quality is job one and one of its most successful dealers maintains that customer satisfaction is job one, facilities management organizations would do well to ensure that both quality and customer service are job one. Employees need to understand that quality and customer service must be a priority if your organization is to be successful.

A wise man, whose name has not been recorded by history, once aptly summed up the concept of service with this advice: "Aim for service, not success, and success will follow."

Handling Customer Complaints

It's too bad that we don't live in a perfect world. A world where everything goes right all the time; where nothing ever wears out, breaks down or gets out of adjustment; where everyone does their job and does it right the first time; where there are no emergencies, and plenty of time is allotted for completing the work; where the price charged is always right; and where resources are always adequate to do the job that needs to be done.

But things do go wrong, systems fail, and people don't always do the job right the first time, so every now and then you will receive criticisms. Criticisms can come to anyone in an organization whether on the top or bottom of the totem pole. Most of us resent criticism. We tend to take criticism personally and sometimes overreact to complaints.

Many times our customers fail to realize that the world is not perfect—and neither are its systems, its equipment, or its people. Even so, because the facilities management unit is a service organization, customers expect, and even demand, the best service available. When service does not meet their expectations, the complaints will follow. Whether or not customer service is specifically your job (and whose job doesn't have an aspect of customer service?), here are some helpful, universal guidelines to keep in mind.

Answer Promptly. This includes not just picking up the phone quickly but quickly getting a satisfactory answer to a question or taking prompt action to resolve a problem. Customers don't like to wait for extended periods of time to receive answers, responses, and actions.

Get All the Facts. Don't "yes" the customer and hang up before you find out what's really wrong. If you are interrupted from one job to another by a customer with a question or concern, take the time to get their full story and jot down some notes for follow up. Without the right information and timely follow up, you'll just waste your time and irritate the customer.

Admit Mistakes. This one's a bit tougher because you don't want to admit to a mistake if one hasn't really been made. But if you installed the bookshelf in the wrong office, or repaired the wrong vehicle, don't insist that the customer made the mistake. If there was an error made, admit it (even if it you are not personally responsible) and do what must be done to correct the matter.

Don't Argue. If the mistake was indeed made by the customer but the customer denies it, there is little accomplished in resolving the matter by arguing with them. The only thing the customer wants (and will accept) is to have the job or desired work done as it was anticipated. After all, if we can keep the customer happy, it really doesn't matter in the grand scheme of universal happenings if they were right or wrong.

Be Polite. With some customers, especially if they are irate or sarcastic, this can be a challenge. The true test of a professional, however, is to remain calm and express unfailing courtesy. Politeness can have a calming effect on even the most annoying customer.

Always Leave the Customer Satisfied. Even though it may require an additional measure of effort, try to resolve customer issues and concerns in a manner that will give total satisfaction. Sometimes it may be tempting to arrange the easiest possible solution, but that may not be the best long-term fix. A satisfied customer is a good ally to have.

As a service organization, the facilities management unit can only be successful if its employees continually strive to keep customers happy. No matter how efficient and cost effective you are in managing the physical plant resources of the institution, in the end you are judged by what your customers think and say about you. If you are selective in which customers you cater to or if you are inconsistent in attempts to resolve complaints, you will never be viewed as a good customer-focused organization. Your willingness to put forth a little extra time and effort to resolve customer concerns and to make the customer happy will pay great dividends, not only for the facilities organization, but for you as an individual as well.

Communication is the Key

That's Not My Job

One of the most frustrating responses a person can have to a reported problem or need is for someone to tell them, "That's not my job," or "That's not in my department." The person making the call is usually already feeling some urgency about the matter or they wouldn't have bothered to call. Obviously in a case such as this, there is a perceived problem and there are expectations that the problem will be solved.

The facilities department should be the "problem solver" on campus and not a part of the problem. There's a feeling on most campuses that "if you don't know who to call, call facilities." People look to your department to solve their problems. If something needs to be done, should assist in getting the job done even if it isn't technically your job.

When something needs to be done, a good employee-at any level-doesn't wait to be told to do it. If they have the authority, they should simply go ahead and do it. If there's any doubt whether they have the authority to act, they should point out the problem, suggest action, and ask for approval. If it's completely out of their area, they should tactfully recommend action to those who do have the authority.

The point is that if something needs to be done, the person with initiative feels a personal responsibility to do what he or she can to get it started. The person without initiative may be just as willing to work hard, and just as able, but they don't have the spark to start action on their own. A person who has to be told each and every thing to do throughout the day is not a very valuable employee.

Why do some people hesitate to take the responsibility for changing anything or for starting in new directions? There are many reasons, one of which is fear of being blamed if the project fails. Another reason-and perhaps the most unfortunate one-is that they simply don't see the problem as a part of their job.

Good employees have to be self-starters. They anticipate the needs of their job and don't expect their supervisors to do it for them. They see what needs doing and do it without waiting to be prompted. They accept responsibility for developing new ideas and methods-within the limits of their authority-without waiting to be prodded.

Any employee who wants to be successful is particularly interested in advancement, must realize that they are paid to think and to take care of those things that show up wherever their job takes them. That's what being a good employee does. It's what the institution, boss, coworkers, and everyone else looks to them for. If you don't take initiative, you aren't doing your job.

Don't get so specialized in what you do that you

can't take the necessary action, whenever and wherever needed, to get anything within your means done. Be the solution, not the problem! That is your job.

The Key to Customer Service

You Are the Department

A customer walks into the reception area of a facilities management building. No one was around and so the customer had to wait. A clerk from the service center walked by on her way to the copy room. She could have kept going, but instead she stopped and asked, "May I help you?"

The customer explained that he was trying to locate one of the managers. The clerk diverted from her original destination long enough to place a quick phone call to the manager. The manager asked her to direct the customer to his office. The customer was pleased and later told three people about the clerk who had stopped to help him. "She didn't have to do that because it wasn't her job," he said. "But she helped me, and I was in a hurry. The people in that department must really look out for their customers."

To be successful, facilities management departments must operate just like any other company that offers service as its main product. Successful companies know that customers form an impression of them on the basis of each

Communication is the Key

encounter with their employees. That's why it is important to treat every customer contact as a moment of truth, a time when relationships can be made or broken, a time when impressions are made, either good or bad.

To a customer, you are the department, no matter what your job is. Customers will come away from every encounter feeling either happy or dissatisfied, and that's how they will think of the department until the next encounter with one of your employees. Each employee within facilities management needs to ask themselves the following questions:

1. Who are my customers?
2. What are their needs?
3. What are their expectations?
4. What services do I have to offer?
5. How does my service meet their needs and expectations?
6. How can I better serve my customers?

As each of us is able to answer these questions, we are better able to see our place and what is expected of us within the department.

You are a very important person in your department. In every customer encounter you have the power to influence customers. Realize that what you do matters. Sometimes you don't even need to come in contact with the customer. They judge the department from the evidence of your presence in your work results. That work can be a clean office, a comfortable temperature, a light fixture that now works, a vehicle that is clean and full of fuel, or shrubs that have been trimmed away from the sidewalk.

The Key to Customer Service

A careless word, an indifferent attitude, or a thoughtless act can ruin a customer relationship forever. On the other hand, if you are helpful, enthusiastic, and concerned, people will be impressed with you and the department that you represent.

You have the power to make the department successful or not, based on how you treat people. Be concerned with excellence. Treat customers royally, whenever you encounter them. Whenever possible, you need to give your customers clear signals that they are important to you. You should make them feel good at every opportunity.

And recognize that because *you* are the department, you are important.

Communication is the Key

How Good is Your Service?

Time magazine once featured a cover story entitled "Why Is Service So Bad?" and the subtitle read "Puleeze! Will Somebody Help Me?" The entire article dealt with the plight of frustrated American consumers who wonder where the service went. It seems that more and more customers are feeling extremely frustrated since personal service has become a "maddeningly" rare commodity in the American marketplace. Thomas Peters, a management consultant and coauthor of the book, *In Search Of Excellence*, has concluded that, "in general, service in America stinks."

The popular film *Back to the Future* cracked up its audiences with a scene in which Michael J. Fox's character, who traveled back in time, walks past a 1950s-era filling station and is flabbergasted to see four cheery attendants in neatly pressed overalls. Like a pit crew at the Indy 500, they dash up to a car and proceed to fill the gas tank, check the oil, clean the windows, and polish the chrome. Americans tolerated and even welcomed self-service during an era of rising prices, but now a backlash has taken place. The result is that some companies are scrambling to make amends, and "quality of service" is the current business buzz phrase.

The *Time* article maintains that the simple reason customer service workers have so little attention to give is that businesses often overwork them to save labor costs and keep prices low. The article also concludes that too many service workers lack any pride or satisfaction in their jobs, especially in a society like America's, which puts so much emphasis on speedy upward mobility.

You are probably asking yourself: what does this have to do with the operations of a facilities management organization? While that article in *Time* dealt exclusively with problems in retail businesses, there are lessons to be learned that can benefit the facilities professional.

Lesson #1: The same people that are unhappy with the lack of service from the retail community will also be unhappy with the facilities management organization if it is not service oriented. After all, the facilities management unit is supposed to be a service organization. Even though we fight some of the same problems as retailers, too few people and too few dollars to go around, we still must provide the service.

Lesson #2: While the magazine article suggests that too many service workers in retail lack pride and satisfaction in their jobs, it is gratifying to observe in many instances the pride and satisfaction exhibited by facilities management employees. A campus could not function as well as it does or look as good as it does without employees who take pride in doing their jobs and in return, receive satisfaction from knowing they have done a good job. If you ever lose these qualities, your department will be in serious trouble.

Lesson #3: Quality of service does get noticed. Facilities managers who incorporate customer service into their organizational culture regularly receive notes and letters from all across campus telling them how the services provided by the facilities organization are appreciated. The facilities operations can be successful only by providing services that satisfy its "customers," which are the students, faculty, and staff at the institution.

How good is your service? It can only be as good as each employee makes it. Hopefully, no one will ever say, "Why is service so bad?" in reference to your department. That can never happen as long as you and your staff still care.

Instead, be sure customers say, "Their service is great!" after dealing with your facilities management organization.

Section III

Key Tips for Facilities Professionals

Communication is the Key

What is a Professional?

For many years I have been convinced of the need for all facilities management employees to function as professionals. There can be professionalism at all levels within your organization. If your department is to be successful as a service unit, it is imperative that every custodian, every carpenter, every grounds worker, every plumber, and indeed every employee, function as a professional within their own field. Being an integral part of a university or school, your work within a professional environment cannot afford to be anything less than professional.

Some people have asked me, "What do you mean by saying that facilities management employees should be professionals?" and "How do you define a professional?"

My wife has heard my remarks about professionalism, particularly during my time as president of the Association of Physical Plant Administrators of Universities and Colleges (now APPA: The Association of Higher Education Facilities Officers), and she found a definition of professionalism that is strikingly similar:

> Professionalism is not a gift.
> It is a wage earned by
> education, effort, performance,
> and commitment.

However, professionalism implies not only competence, but also the manner in which work is done.

An industry colleague heard my remarks about professionalism at an APPA regional meeting and shared with me his own definition of what constitutes a professional: "When we call someone a 'professional' we are complimenting that person for possessing many attributes. A professional is an expert, one who has mastered a body of knowledge and is competent in a particular field. A professional who is committed to his or her field is committed to truth. We admire professionals, and we need them. We admire them for their specialized knowledge and competence, and we need them to live in a world made dizzy by a continuous explosion of knowledge.

"Yet when we approvingly assign the word 'professional' to someone, we are speaking of more than knowledge, more than just talent, more than expertise. We are speaking of someone who is able to take that knowledge, talent, and expertise, and use them well. A professional is one who both listens to the truth and acts on the truth. In the quality of that action is measured the quality of the professional."

True professionals will find quality ways of getting the job done.

If you agree and understand these definitions of professionalism, you are well on your way to being a professional employee.

Moments of Truth

Each of us in our personal lives experiences incidents that tend to be "moments of truth." These moments arise when you must make a difficult decision or ethical judgment, when a personal tragedy hits, or when faced with a medical crisis. During these occasions, you are called upon to take decisive action, make timely decisions, or convey appropriate remarks that reveal your "real" self. These moments of truth identify you and what you truly believe, what you stand for as a person, and how you measure up. In the same manner, every business or organization that provides a service or product has similar moments of truth with its customers.

Moments of truth vary from business to business and from organization to organization. For a retail establishment, a moment of truth happens when the customer asks a sales clerk for assistance. For a bakery, the moment of truth happens when the customer bites into its product. The moment of truth for a nurse is how painless a shot can be administered. Moments of truth happen within every organization on a continuous basis.

For each of you in a facilities management organization that moment of truth comes when you answer the telephone, personally greet a departmental secretary, clean an office, adjust a thermostat, or in a hundred-and-one other tasks you probably perform each day. During these brief encounters with your customers (students, staff, faculty, and visitors), they are exposed to what you do and how you do it. As a facilities management organization, your services touch each and every person that comes and goes (or even stays) on campus. How you respond—directly or indirectly—to your customers determines how they feel about the organization. And, to a degree, how they feel about your school, college, or university.

Consider the following universal moments of truth:

How fast and how well the phones are answered. Unanswered phones that ring and ring, and curt or unhelpful responses once they are answered, turn people off or make them angry. Prompt answering of phones and courteous and friendly responses make for satisfied customers.

The appearance and cleanliness of the buildings and grounds. While people sometimes blame an inadequate budget for less than desirable conditions, you can typically make the difference, more so than the dollars spent. Instances can be cited where two maintenance organizations were provided nearly identical resources and yet the condition of the facilities at one institution was far superior to the other. Why the difference? It was the work of a motivated and caring staff.

The appearance of employees. The appearance of individuals creates initial impressions that go beyond just having neat and clean clothing and good grooming. The demeanor an individual carries with them can tell the customer a lot about that person. An employee that enjoys what he or she is doing demonstrates that attitude in their appearance. The opposite is also true.

Whether employees smile and appear to be pleasant. On occasion, each of us may have been accused of being "mad" at someone because we failed to smile at them. Smiles and a pleasant demeanor are important to your customers.

How promptly customers are helped or served. When considering this item, we typically think in terms of retail establishments, but there are parallels within the facilities management organization. Some examples: Do you promptly return telephone calls? Are routine trouble calls addressed in a timely manner? How long does one wait to have an overly hot room restored to an acceptable temperature?

How routine customer questions are handled. How you address complaints, trouble calls, project and billing status inquiries, and so forth, is critically important. Facilities departments deal with a wide variety of technical issues on a daily basis, and your customers should not be expected to understand the technical side of operations, but many times inquiries are made because someone needs to know or is genuinely interested. Respond to those inquiries in a timely and friendly manner.

The cleanliness of restrooms. The greater part of a building might be spotless, but a dirty restroom leaves a bad overall impression of the facility, as well as of the maintenance operation.

The effectiveness of signs. Many institutions have committed considerable time and resources to develop and maintain an attractive and effective system of signage. Signs are critical from a wayfinding standpoint. Signage should not only help first-time visitors find the campus, but should also help them find parking, a particular building, and then a room within the building.

How problems are handled. Problems will always arise even though you make concerted efforts to prevent them. Just as important as preventing problems, however, is how you respond to them when they do occur. Problems should always be addressed in a professional manner.

In your own organization, pay attention to what happens when these "moments of truth" occur. Your responses will put both the facilities management organization and the institution in a favorable light.

Key Tips for Facilities Professionals

Put Your 'Know-How' to Work

The story is told about a farmer who listened patiently to an overly enthusiastic salesperson leafing through a thick manual on scientific farming. When asked if he was interested in purchasing the manual, the farmer drawled, "Son, I don't farm half as good as I know how to already."

How many times have you done something that didn't work out, then kicked yourself afterwards because you had known better all along? It happens to the best of us. Arthur Motley, former U.S. Chamber of Commerce president, observed, "Few people are smart enough to remember all they know."

Some people have the knack for doing the right thing instinctively. But for the rest of us, it takes conscious effort to stop and think before acting. For example, the person who remembers to set an example in the little things, like getting to work on time, usually finds others following suit.

You know these things. You can't benefit from the knowledge, however, until is put it into practice. There is a vast storehouse of knowledge that exists within the employees of facilities management departments. You may be a walking encyclopedia on how to be an effective custodian, carpenter, or groundskeeper, but if you don't apply what you know, what use is it?

Sometimes people don't use what they know because they don't stop to think. Others let their emotions get the best of their reason. And a few simply do what is expedient at the moment, even if it may not be the best way to operate in the long run.

Good employees never stop learning how to do their jobs better, but they also concentrate on putting their "know-how" to work. One of the ways facilities departments can survive doing more with less is to use the knowledge that employees collectively possess, enabling you to do things right the first time.

Personally Inspected By Mary

One day I made a purchase in a store and the items were placed in a brown paper bag. Upon reaching home and removing the items from the bag, I happened to notice a stamped message on the bottom, which read, "Personally Inspected by Mary." There was another stamped message below the first, which read, "With Pride from the Best People."

As I read these two messages I tried to envision Mary inspecting each and every brown paper bag that passed her workstation. To some people, checking the quality of paper bags would seem to be a menial and boring job. But as evidenced by the stamped message, Mary takes great pride in her work and wants the whole world to know that she does her job well. She is proud enough to give her name rather than using an identification code such as, "Inspected by No. 21."

The message, "Personally Inspected By Mary," leads me to conclude that if someone can feel pride in inspecting brown paper bags, every employee should take pride in what they do. Whether it be cleaning toilet rooms, raking leaves, changing fan filters, typing letters, or digging a trench, there is something to be said for doing a job.

An attractive campus with well-kept and maintained buildings and grounds doesn't just happen. Many colleges, universities, and schools have many resources to operate and maintain their campuses, and yet the place is a mess! The grounds are littered, and the plant materials show signs of neglect. The buildings, in many cases, are even worse. They are dirty and have the appearance of being old and run down.

What's the difference? The difference is people who care and take pride in their work. Each person needs to learn the same secret that many others have learned. This "secret" is as old as life itself. It is a secret only because it is so big and obvious that we often overlook it in search of something more mysterious and complex. The secret is this: forget about getting, and give!

Crafted By K. Minish

Since finding the message "Personally Inspected by Mary," I have started to look at the bottom of paper bags more often. Some people may question the sanity of someone who goes around reading messages on the bottom of brown paper bags, but I find it interesting. A couple of weeks after discovering Mary's message, I ran across another message that caught my attention. This most recent find on the bottom of a brown paper bag read, "Crafted by K. Minish."

Now, in my opinion, this message is even more significant. K. Minish wants the whole world to know that he is proud of the brown paper bag that he crafts, whereas Mary was only responsible for the inspection of the item. K. Minish is responsible for the fabrication and quality of the bag itself. I was once again impressed that someone like K. Minish could find satisfaction and take pride in constructing something so humble as a brown paper bag. I can even envision K. Minish going home after work and bragging to his wife and family that on that day he had made

Communication is the Key

5,240 bags without one bad bag in the whole lot.

In addition to the obvious message printed on the bottom of this sack, there is an unwritten message there as well. The unwritten message is that people want to feel good about what they do. People want the kind of work in which they can take pride. And people want to let other people know that they do good work.

It is obvious to me that the same pride and satisfaction as exhibited by Mary and K. Minish exists within the minds and attitudes of anyone who maintains and operates physical facilities.

Even though you may not be able to leave your name on the areas or equipment operated and maintained by you, you can leave a mark. Your "mark" can be a clean restroom; it can be a piece of equipment that is clean and well-oiled; it can be a litter-free playfield; it can be a fresh coat of paint; it can be a thermostat that controls the room temperature at the right setting.

Your mark can be all these things and much more. The collective "mark" of a good facilities management operation is how well their facilities are operated and maintained. Each of you has the opportunity to leave your mark on the work you do. Make sure that your mark is left on something to be proud of.

Criticism

None of us gets through life without being criticized every now and then. As employees of a facilities management organization this may be doubly true since your activities are not just limited to your own area of expertise, but affect every student, staff, and faculty member within the institution where you work.

It is also true that most of us resent criticism. We tend to take criticism personally and sometimes overreact not unlike a horse stung by a wasp. Our immediate reaction is to strike out and hit back even when the criticism may be justified.

Some people have developed the art of knowing how to criticize tactfully, but most do not. That is something over which we seem to have little or no control. But each of us needs to learn to accept criticism in a mature fashion, however it is delivered. We can learn to control our own reactions and respond to our critics in an intelligent and professional manner.

The person who doesn't allow himself or herself to

be blinded by resentment can sometimes find good in even the most malicious criticism. If the critic, no matter how unfriendly, points out some weakness you were not aware of, and you take action to correct it, you will have turned the intended "injury" into a genuine benefit.

We shouldn't pretend to be perfect. None of us ought to be naïve enough to think that we never make mistakes and should not be overly sensitive when someone points out these mistakes to us. A present-day philosopher said, "The only nice thing about being imperfect is the joy it brings to others." Most of us have to make mistakes to learn some of life's most valuable lessons. I have many areas that could stand improvement and I don't think I stand alone in this situation. Never be too angry to take help wherever you find it.

Sometimes it's obvious that criticism is unjustified, and intended to wound rather than heal. But it is usually not necessary to accept the challenge and become embroiled in bitter recriminations.

Nothing deflates a critic faster than to accept the criticism as a friendly gesture, and to try to get some good out of it. An ancient Chinese proverb teaches us that "if you are patient in one moment of anger, you will escape a hundred days of sorrow." These are good words to live by.

Key Tips for Facilities Professionals

Why Integrity Matters

When something is complete within itself, possessing an inner strength and soundness, we say it has integrity. And we trust it.

Take for instance a new bridge being constructed. Before the bridge is finished, a flood of storm water flowing down the river channel causes the partially finished bridge to collapse. Its structural integrity is lacking. The finished bridge that was eventually rebuilt did have the needed structural strength and integrity. Over the years, it has passed the critical test of holding up under the weight of the vehicles crossing it and the water flowing against its supporting structure. It has been designed to withstand floods, harsh weather conditions and the constant vibration of vehicular traffic. Its foundations are solid and the pressure points have been strengthened.

But what if the builders of the bridge had substituted a poorer quality of material? Or what if they had made significant deviations from the size and quantity of reinforcing steel? What if they failed to make the right measurements because they ran out of time? In short, what if their own personal integrity was lacking?

In that case, both the bridge and its builders would eventually fail, and the results would have been catastrophic for each.

We probably can't give a person a higher compliment than to say that he or she has integrity. It is a keystone virtue that encompasses both honesty and trustworthiness. And it is a sad moment when we conclude that a person we're dealing with lacks integrity, which is the foundation of good character.

The essential fact of integrity is that no one can give it to us. We cannot inherit it, and we certainly can't buy it. We have to earn it, and the process is a long one that allows very few second chances. It's a trait that almost has to be tested to be perceived, because the world is full of people who claim to have integrity but their actions say otherwise. We learn to be wary of people who claim to be honest until we see them actually being honest.

It is heartening to realize that because integrity is such a personal attribute, anyone can attain it, no matter our individual circumstances of wealth, creed, or origin. Whatever our character is, we have a hand in creating it. The key to integrity is consistency—not only setting high personal standards for oneself (honesty, responsibility, respect for others, fairness) but also living up to these standards each day.

It seems that in every walk of life we run into stories of dishonesty. They include professional people charging prohibitive prices for their services, tap water sold as costly bottled spring water, a few cents of medication selling for many dollars, improper billing practices, workers who steal company time, employers who take advantage of their employees, merchants selling inferior goods, merchandise marked up before being put on sale, rents arbitrarily raised, and so forth.

We can easily spot the characteristics of someone with integrity. They're honest. They do the right thing when nobody is watching. They keep their word and they keep confidences. They repay their debts, and they clean up their own messes. They accept responsibility for their actions. They are calm and untroubled because they know that the decisions they make are based on time-honored principles that they've made a personal commitment to follow.

They understand the Law of the Harvest: Whatever a man soweth, that shall he reap. So plant wisely.

Long ago, the French dramatist Moliere commented wryly that if everyone were clothed with integrity, and if every heart were just, frank and kindly, then we wouldn't need the other virtues. They only exist to make us bear with patience the injustices of others.

We all have a common stake in our place of work, our community, and our society. Our actions do matter. It is essential that we act with integrity in order to build the kind of world in which we all would like to live.

Good Intentions

In the movie *Field of Dreams*, there is a scene that captures a very human situation that we have all experienced. The hero of the movie is sent on a quest to find a baseball player who had played the game many years ago before. This player had the unenviable distinction of holding the worst record in the major leagues. He played in only one game and had zero hits at bat.

When the hero finds him, the ballplayer is an old man. When this former player was interviewed, he was asked what it was like to play in that one single game and how it happened. The old player's response was simple: He had just been called up from the minor leagues, it was the last day of the season, the bottom of the eighth inning and his team was way ahead. The coach suddenly sent him in to play for what turned out to be just one inning. The game ended, the season was over, and he was sent back to the minor leagues, never to see major league play again.

In speaking of his feelings about the situation, the old man said, "I didn't think much of it. We don't recognize the most significant moments of our lives when they're happening. They brush on past you. We think there will be other days...I didn't realize that this would be the only day." Deeply disappointed, he left the game of baseball.

Life is full of moments like that. We are often at crossroads in our lives that can determine widely different directions. Some of the moments we recognize as significant: we leave home, go off to school, move to another town, get another job. These are the events in our lives that we can control and even prepare for. But what of the moments that we don't recognize?

These unrecognized moments are particularly painful when they involve personal relationships. We part company with someone we care for, and later realize we won't ever see him or her again. Life goes on. One of them moves unexpectedly, or they fall ill, or they just drift away. And we never told them how much they meant to us, or how we valued their friendship or how they had served as an example to help us better our own life. In everyone's life there are three things that never return: the past, a neglected opportunity, and the spoken word.

And it isn't just with people that this happens. What about those jobs we promised to do, but haven't gotten around to doing them? What of the little gift or favor we meant to send, but didn't? Or the letter we haven't answered? Most of us have things waiting for us just as soon as we get time for them. We become very good at delaying things, often until they can't be done at all.

If we live life with a pattern of putting things off, we're destined to do a lot of wishing: wishing that we had taken advantage of the moment when it was there; wishing that we had finished the job that we started; wishing we had given up that bad habit earlier; wishing we had told our family and friends that we cared for them while there was still time to do it.

The message here is this: When you seen an opportunity to do good, just do it. And do it now. Delay is the enemy of good intentions. When you think of a nice thing to do for someone, don't just think it, do it.

When you have a kind thought, express it. If you admire something someone has said or done, speak up and say so. You will both be the better for it.

In *Field of Dreams*, which is just a fictional story after all, the old ballplayer gets another chance to play, and wouldn't we all like to have that same opportunity.

But that's not what happens in real life. As Conrad Aiken once wrote, "One ought to see everything that one has a chance of seeing; because in life not many have one chance and none has two." And Dale Carnegie once observed, "One of the most tragic things I know about human nature is that all of us tend to put off living. We are all dreaming of some magical rose garden over the horizon—instead of enjoying the roses that are blooming outside our window today." Life should focus more on the journey rather than the destination.

Now would be a good time to fulfill all those good intentions you've been hoarding. Too often we underestimate the impact of a touch, a smile, a kind word, a listening ear, an honest compliment, or the smallest act of caring, all of which have the potential to turn a life around. Just do it!

Discount Maintenance is No Bargain

Everyone likes a bargain, right? When it comes to buildings and their systems maintenance, however, it may be well to heed the advice of John Ruskin, English author, art critic, and social reformer, who said, "It is unwise to pay too much, but it is worse to pay too little. The common law of business balance prohibits paying a little and getting a lot…it can't be done. When you deal with the lowest bidder, it is wise to add something for the risk you run, and if you do that you will have enough to pay for something better!"

This simple fact regarding cost was written over 100 years ago and is as true today as it was then. John Ruskin would have made a darn good facilities manager. I have another of his statements hanging on my office wall: "There is hardly anything in the world that some man cannot make a little worse and sell a little cheaper, and the people who consider price only are this man's lawful prey." I have found that this bit of sage advice can come in handy when an irate customer drops by to complain about costs.

Communication is the Key

There are oodles of companies and contractors who claim to offer discount building and systems maintenance services for schools, colleges, and universities. The claim is that services can be provided "cheaper" than the costs for doing the same work with in-house staff. In reality, many of these companies perform what might be termed "breakdown maintenance."

What happens is this: the facilities manager calls for service (oftentimes, it is an emergency situation). The "discount" company or contractor sends someone out to patch things up, and the facilities manager is led to believe that everything is working fine. A short time later the system fails again, and this cycle continues until the system is in such bad shape that it must be replaced. Now the facilities manager, through no fault of his or her own (except for using the "discount" company in the first place), is faced with a large unexpected expense. And guess who's standing at the front of the line to cash in on the misfortune? The same company or contractor who's been offering "discount" service.

Maintaining buildings, along with their complex mechanical, electrical, and controls systems, in such a manner is like putting a bandage on a cancer. Without routine preventive maintenance and routine testing procedures, there is no way of knowing what trouble lies ahead. Most automobile owners would not think of continually driving their vehicles without changing the oil, greasing the fittings, checking the tire pressure, fan belts, and the coolant. Sometimes when it comes to a building's mechanical and electrical systems—which are obviously more complex and represent a much larger investment than the family car-those in control of budgets sometimes fail to realize that these systems will not perform adequately if preventive and routine maintenance services are ignored.

Maintenance staff who know they must fix the system when it breaks down, usually are more caring, more attentive, and more interested in keeping things running than in making costly repairs after the system fails. Maintaining a cadre of well-trained and skilled workers is essential to well-maintained facilities. Somewhere within the facilities management operation there needs to be an "institutional memory," and that cannot reside within rotating contracted services.

All of this assumes that maintenance budgets are at least minimally adequate to do the job. That may not be a valid assumption in all cases. But whether the work is accomplished through outsourcing or with in-house staff, an inadequate budget will result in rapidly deteriorating buildings and systems.

I suspect that most facilities managers are in favor of free enterprise, but I question whether or not the wholesale outsourcing of building and system maintenance will produce well-maintained buildings in the long run. Firms that live and die by the profit motive, usually do not think in the same long-term manner as the in-house staff does.

While there are numerous instances where well-managed outsourcing can benefit the facilities manager, as a general rule "privatization" of building maintenance services will never receive the same degree of attention and dedication as that provided by in-house career-oriented staff. I make this statement knowing full well that there are exceptions to every rule.

So, do you still want to save money on bargain maintenance provided by a "discount" company or contractor? I don't think so.

Setting and Achieving Goals

In the book *Alice's Adventures in Wonderland*, Alice learns a lesson in goal setting. Alice meets a Cheshire cat at a crossroads and asks, "Would you tell me, please, which way I ought to go from here?" The Cheshire cat says, "Depends a good deal on where you want to get to." Alice replies, "I don't much care where," to which the cat replies, "Then it doesn't matter which way you go."

Several years ago while driving on the freeway, I noticed three hitchhikers waiting near an on-ramp to receive a ride. Each of them carried a homemade sign, which announced his desired destination. One sign read "Los Angeles" while a second sign carried the destination "Boise." However, it was the third sign, which not only caught my attention, but caused me to ponder and reflect its message. The third hitchhiker was not trying to reach Los Angeles, California, nor Boise, Idaho, but on the cardboard sign it read simply "ANYWHERE."

Here was a person content to travel in any direction, according to the whim of the driver who stopped to give him a free ride. What an enormous price to pay for such a ride. No plan. No objective. No goal. The road to "anywhere" is the road to nowhere, and the road to nowhere leads to dreams sacrificed, opportunities squandered, and a life unfulfilled.

Imagine yourself where you will be ten years from now. Think about what you will be doing, and the person you would be if your highest hopes and dreams came true. Think about your personal goals such as: I want to finish my education and graduate from college; I want to be the best craft worker in my field; I want to raise my level of spirituality. One needs to carefully think about what they really want to do, and think about what they really want to be. Short-range goals need to be set. Short-range goals are merely stepping stones that will lead to the accomplishment of long-range accomplishments.

An old Chinese proverb makes this point well, "A journey of a thousand miles begins with a single step." There are four recognized steps that may be followed in order to properly set and achieve goals.

Step 1. Decide what needs to be done. Make a list of the things you would like to know, qualities and abilities you would like to possess, and things you want to have happen in your life or you want to accomplish.

Step 2. Decide what to do and when to do it. Write down the goal and how you plan to reach it. Remember, a goal not written down is merely a "wish." Choose some friend, family member, or a person to whom you will report the progress you make. Set a time to complete your goals, and date check your progress along the way.

Step 3. Act on your plan. If the goal is something

you can do by yourself, do it! If you need help, ask someone to help you.

Step 4. Report your progress and results. Meet with the person to whom you chose to report your progress. Tell them what you have done, and check your progress. Some of your goals may be confidential and need not be shared with another person.

After you have completed Step 4, begin the process again by evaluating what needs to be done next. If you are at a crossroads and don't really know which way to go, sit down and follow the steps previously outlined. You may be surprised at what you can accomplish or what you can be if you take the time to plan out your destination.

Section IV

The Key to Leadership and Change

Pursuit of Excellence

We can learn much from the experiences of great performers and great people. There are some acts of greatness and exemplary lives that so inspire the general population that there is almost unanimous accord about their heroic stature. One of the traits admired by the people of nations with a history of "frontier" is that of endurance—a quality that still reminds us of the basic struggle with nature and unknown perils. Throughout history, these individuals have stood out for their bravery, firmness, or greatness of soul.

Notable heroes have also emerged from the ranks of those who have been trailblazers and pioneers in a particular field of endeavor. In some cases, individuals have had to achieve international recognition before people in their own country would acknowledge them.

Sports figures have long been universally admired in popular culture, where often we are reluctant to idolize other achievers, but our adulation has often been fickle and short-lived. The light generated by most sports stars shines brightly but briefly. Yesterday's athletes are quickly forgotten along with the sports that made them famous. Others continue to be remembered.

For instance, the feats of Louis Cyr, a Quebec strongman, are still recounted today. Late in the nineteenth century, Louis Cyr, the "Amazing Canadian," was a person who never backed down from a challenge and was undefeated in feats of strength. He remains a legend to this day.

The legend began in his teens when Cyr, who inherited his strength from his mother, allegedly pulled a loaded farm wagon out of the mud by lifting it on his back. In 1895, he again used his back to lift 4,337 pounds, perhaps his greatest feat.

Cyr's fame was earned before accurate records were kept, and before weight lifting was included among Olympic events. In any event, Cyr's record remains uncontested and incontestable.

Defeat weighs heavily when a goal nearly attained suddenly slips beyond one's grip. Perhaps athletes know this better than others. Clifton Cushman was one of America's promising athletes, who set a record in high school that still stands after more than 40 years. At the 1960 Olympic Games, he won the silver medal in the 400-meter hurdles and seemed assured of a gold medal in the next games. During the American Trials for the 1964 Olympics, however, he tripped over a hurdle and was eliminated. In response to messages of condolence, he wrote an open letter to the youth of his hometown in Grand Forks, North Dakota.

In this letter, Cushman wrote, "In a split second all the many years of training, pain, sweat, blister, and agony of running were simply and irrevocably wiped out. But I tried. I would much rather fail knowing I had put forth an honest effort than never to have tried at all."

Cushman never got the chance to make another attempt at his Olympic goal. In 1966, he was listed as missing in action in Vietnam and then in 1975 the U.S. Department of Defense officially declared him as presumed killed in action.

Of course not everyone is capable of great feats of strength or has the ability of make an Olympic team, but there is nothing preventing you from trying to reach your goals, whether in sports, education, a job, or whatever else you pursue. Everyone should have goals.

Few endeavors warrant more respect than the pursuit of excellence. Some people make little effort to raise their sights and pursue a difficult goal. Perhaps knowing that few are able to achieve difficult goals, some elect never to make the attempt at all. They guarantee that they won't be faced with failure by not making any attempt at all.

Many (perhaps most) people fear challenges and problems. But facing challenges, even if you don't always meet them, often leads to your greatest growth. Failure frequently leads you to opportunities that might have been missed in more successful circumstances. It is the old adage that "necessity is the mother of invention."

If you take advantage of opportunities as they arise, you are pursuing excellence. At that point, you can see progress and, with confidence, successfully move on to greater accomplishments. Growth and strength come as you face and wrestle with challenges. Avoiding them only makes you weaker. Life is not about avoiding challenges, but rather what you do to overcome them. If you regularly face up to challenges and problems, and view them as opportunities, the process becomes easier and more natural. If you refuse to accept anything but the best, you get it more often.

Whatever role you play within your own facilities management organization, you should not fear or shun challenges. Your best opportunities may come from facing problems head-on and satisfactorily resolving them.

Aristotle, the Greek philosopher, maintained that excellence is an act won by training and habituation. One does not act rightly because of inherent virtue or excellence, but rather because one has acted rightly. Therefore, excellence is a habit.

The difference between ordinary and extraordinary is sometimes no more than that little bit of extra effort.

Communication is the Key

Staying Focused

I grew up in a rural area in Idaho when the technology of farming was evolving from an era of hard manual labor to a more mechanized mode of operation. The locality was spotted with small family farms, unlike the mega-tracts found under cultivation today.

Typical to each farm was a pasture, most of which were quite generous in size. One particular pasture in the area was about five acres in size and was home to a small flock of sheep, guarded by a feisty and seemingly fearless ram.

As youngsters sometimes do, it was not uncommon for those who knew about the ram to dare those who didn't know to walk across the pasture. The ram, ever protective his flock, or perhaps just looking for a little action, would chase the intruder and butt them to the ground. Even though many tried, not even those adept at broken-field running could avoid getting caught. All were overtaken and knocked down by the ram.

Knowing the ram's disposition, these youngsters

should have known better than to send unsuspecting friends (or even those they disliked) into the fray. A very questionable practice, but they did.

Maybe because the pasture provided a shortcut to the only country store for miles around, the deceptive youngsters-ever searching for a shorter route to the source of chocolate candy and soda pop-continually searched for a way to get them safely through the pasture. They operated under the motto that trying times are not the times to stop trying. Eventually, they discovered something quite extraordinary.

Before entering the pasture, the boys would pick the wild grass from the nearby ditch bank, bunch it together into a large bouquet, and hold it high in their hands like an Olympic torch. Then they'd run just like Olympic torch runners: one-by-one across the well-grazed expanse of grass.

The ram, as expected, would take up the chase and, given its superior physical skills, would quickly catch the young men. But the lads, given their superior intellectuals skills, would simply toss the bundles of grass to the ground. The ram, given its inferior reasoning skills, would stop to munch the grass, and the lads would skip off to safety beyond the pasture fence. The hapless ram never did figure out that he could have had his cake (in this case the luckless torchbearer) and eaten it too (the grass). A multitude of lessons, of course, can be learned from these encounters. So let's first consider the not-so-friendly ram.

The ram was originally intent on the noble cause of protecting the flock from intruders. But he was all-too-easily distracted by the lure of an easy meal. He, in short, yielded to satisfying his appetite at the expense of a more noble pursuit.

A ram has no reasoning skills, but you do. This leads to a few questions you might ask yourselves:

- What distracts you from achieving your goals?
- What distractions come along to lessen your enjoyment of life?
- What obstacles keep you from getting rich?
- Simply put, needn't we just maintain our focus on what we want to achieve?

But life, somehow, isn't quite that simple. Obstacles are everywhere. And while there is no way to avoid many of life's obstacles, all too many are self-imposed by the choices you make. Now, let's consider the boys.

The boys, intent on getting those goodies at the country store, would not be distracted by the ram's threats. While, in this particular experience, the goal was certainly trivial, the example is insightful.

In their first attempts to cross the pasture, the boys were knocked down again and again. But sometimes your greatest accomplishments are not achieved in never failing, but in rising every time you fail. Not only did these boys get up and try again, but they also figured out a way to outsmart the enemy. I'm sure that to a degree they did it for excitement, for the thrill of the chase, and for the challenge it posed. The lure of the sweets may have been the initial incentive for their mad dash across the pasture, but outsmarting the ram was also the goal. When they boys first started in their quest to outsmart the ram they had no idea how it could be done. But over time and through the generation of many possible solutions, the desired outcome was finally reached.

For those things you really want out of life, stay focused on the goal and don't get distracted by short-term wants. If you do this, just like the boys in this example, your reward will be the goodies or whatever else you seek.

You don't have to know how you're going to get there, but you need to know where you want to go. It is crucial to have a crystal clear picture of what you want to accomplish. Just as an out-of-focus lens ruins a photograph, your end result will become "fuzzy" if your mental focus is lost. One must operate with a sharply defined mental image of the outcome. Visualize your arrival and the rewards that wait. And just as surely as a magnet is attracted to steel, a solution begins to appear and answers come.

If you start worrying too much about getting from here to there, you are bogged down in the question of methodology. People always seem to get hung up on the "how to" aspects of getting there. Look at it this way: you're not supposed to be concerned about what happens in the middle of a jump, you're supposed to be thinking about where you're going to land!

Communication is the Key

Chronobiology and You

Are you tuned into your staff's daily work rhythms? As a manager, you need to make the most of your staff's energies. Understanding their energies can improve how your office or department functions. The science of chronobiology can provide you with a creative and highly effective tool.

Chronobiology is the study of the complex system of internal body clocks, which tick, in daily, weekly, monthly, and yearly cycles. It is a hard science based on facts, not a speculative one like biorhythms. Understanding chronobiology and working with it can help you to time assignments and take full advantage of your staff's talents. The following information may help you in your planning process.

Morning. Short-term memory is sharpest during early morning hours. If you want your staff to recall statistics, budget figures, or other numbers, ask them in the morning. Your staff will handle other mental exercises better in the late morning. These efforts include those involving complex thinking, organizational skills, and creative problem solving. Ask your workers to write analytical reports during the late morning period. A person's alertness peaks at noon. Morning is also the time when you find your staff in its best mood. No one seems to know why the happiness quotient is highest in the early hours of the day. It may be that happiness is linked to alertness. This time of the day is the best time to maneuver and discipline people. Also it may be the best time for you to handle problems such as a negative performance review.

Mid-Afternoon. A person's long-term memory is best during this time. Schedule any work that requires staff to absorb and remember information. For you that might mean spending time to memorize your speech for requesting a raise from your boss, or a presentation to be made to the president's cabinet. Training sessions are best scheduled after lunch. Creativity, however, will not flow during these hours so don't decide to hold that brainstorming session in the afternoon.

Late Afternoon. The senses—taste, sight, touch, hearing, and smell—are sharpest during late afternoon. Any tasks relying on the use of sensory aptitude or skills will be performed best after 3:00 p.m.

Aside from biological patterns, different individuals on your staff have their own personal work rhythms. Identify what these work rhythms are so that you can get the best performance out of each individual. Here are some features to take into account when working on productivity improvements:

Communication is the Key

- Timing. Some employees accomplish the most during the last hour of the day, others during the first.

- Rituals. Rituals provide clues to peak performance. Watch for repeated behaviors that proceed bursts of concentrated effort. It may be a phone call to the kids at 3:00 p.m., a pencil sharpening binge, or a fresh cup of coffee. Don't mistake these acts for idle time wasters.

- Noise Level. Some workers are distracted by sounds of conversation, music, telephones, and other office noise, while others find it stimulating.

- Weekly Calendar. Some workers accomplish the most at the week's end, others on Monday.

- Pace. A variety of work styles exist: slow and steady versus fast, for example, or juggling four projects simultaneously versus sticking to one task at a time.

- Observation. It is unrealistic for you to expect all employees to work to your rhythm. Tune into theirs. Use differences among your staff to increase your department's productivity.

The Key to Leadership and Change

Human Relations

Under the pressure of getting the work done, educational facilities managers rely heavily upon the technical aspects of operating and maintaining campus facilities and infrastructure. We find ourselves caught up in determining the appropriate response to questions like:

- Is the sequence of the chillers that operate in the central plant providing for optimal plant efficiencies?
- Does the vertical cleaning mode of custodial service provide the best cleaning potential?
- Is the decision to install a single-ply roof the best of all options presented?
- In our remodeling projects, what changes need to be made in our project tracking system to better coordinate the phases of the work and efforts of the trades?

While the impact of technical decisions cannot be minimized in a successful facilities management organization, often it is the human relation's aspect of the job that ultimately determines success or failure. Employees may well have the necessary technical skills to do almost anything that is asked of them, but it is in the process of asking, assigning, motivating, and giving recognition to employees who do the work that the real successes and failures are assured.

Human Relations is the study of human problems arising from organizational and interpersonal relations. I was recently reminded of that subject when I read a few short sentences that combine to form a brief systematic work called "A Short Course in Human Relations." This caused me to reflect upon the study of interpersonal relationships and its application to everyday jobs, even though it is equally applicable to family and other relationships.

The six most important words are "I admit I made a mistake." Since this short course deals with humans, realize that "to err is human" and it should come as no surprise that each of us makes mistakes. The biggest mistake anyone can make is to deny his or her mistake in the first place. As a facilities manager, recognize that mistakes will be made in some of the work that is done by your various departments. Your customers also realize (sometimes begrudgingly) that people make mistakes. Sometimes too much unproductive energy is spent in trying to justify or cover up mistakes. That energy is better spent in resolving the problem. It is far better to admit to mistakes and get on with solutions than to attempt to cover up mistakes and prolong the agony.

The five most important words are "You did a good job." Sometimes when a coworker does a good job, the assumption is that they don't need any acknowledgment. Maybe the one-on-one relationship atmosphere within your organization is such that one must assume that they did a good job unless someone tells them they didn't. Don't rely on these assumptions. You could be wrong. It gives the ego a tremendous boost to actually hear someone say, "You did a good job." It makes people feel better about each other too. Job satisfaction arises from a variety of factors, not the least of which involves the recognition of accomplishments.

The four most important words are "What is your opinion?" Have you ever had the experience of sitting together as a group in a brainstorming session and then using the group's dynamics to solve a problem? If you have, no doubt you have discovered that most people have good ideas. In these instances, you also find that the whole is greater than the sum of the parts or, in other words, a group of people working together can come up with better ideas and solutions to problems than if each person came up with ideas and solutions independently. I view it as an honor to be asked my opinion and others do too. Asking for a person's opinion tells them that they are valued for their ideas and that their opinion matters. Don't ask for opinions, however, if you are not serious about accepting the opinion on its own merits.

The three most important words are "If you please." Civility is best demonstrated through requests rather than demands. Respecting the feelings of others is a common courtesy. Harsh commands and curt demands are rarely found in the same climate where courtesy and civility are present. In describing courteous behavior, one person said,

"Just be nice."

The two most important words are "Thank you." Courtesy includes the use of phrases such as "thank you." The impression that you give to customers, coworkers, and associates is an important part of your job. First of all, it is certainly more pleasant if your coworkers and your supervisor express courtesies to toward you and others. Second, facilities departments have many customers in the form of students, staff, faculty, and visitors to the campus that expect (and should receive) courteous treatment.

The one most important word is "We." Together you and your staff can accomplish a great deal. Together you can make things happen that are impossible through individual or divided efforts. Teams and teamwork cannot exist without two or more individuals. Team accomplishment knows no boundaries, and being part of a team is important.

The least important word is "I." While individualism is important, the person who doesn't think beyond his or her individual needs or interests will offer a limited contribution to their job, their community, or to society, for that matter. Tasks are usually accomplished best by a group effort, and rarely can one person do it all. If we thought only about ourselves, there would be only rare instances of cooperation, significant accomplishment, or progress.

John Donne suggested that "no man [or woman] is an island," and we cannot function alone and apart from the rest of the world. If you heed the lesson taught by these few lines, the tone of your organization would improve and there would be more cooperation, more teamwork, more loyalty, and more "buy-in" of employees. The rewards can be tremendous whether on or off the job. Try it. It works.

Lessons in Leadership

As facilities managers, you may sometimes feel that your lot in life is hard. Being constantly bombarded by the challenges associated with inadequate operating budgets, growing backlogs of deferred maintenance, government mandates without funding, complacency in the workforce, and working within policies and procedures that are bureaucratic in nature, could lead you to conclude that another profession would have been a better choice.

But if you take time to think about some of the global in today's world, the magnitude of your own challenges pales by comparison. Some items that immediately come to mind are:

- The threat of overpopulation and inadequate food supplies;
- The threat of nuclear warfare and terrorism;
- Global warming and its resultant calamities;
- Corrupt government and factional battles that lead to starvation, famine, and plague;

Communication is the Key

- The general degeneration of society as exhibited by increases in violence, racial strife, and poverty.

As you attempt to analyze the challenges facing our planet, as well as those faced in your workday world, the common need is for leaders who have the right vision and who are willing to take charge. You are besieged with theories about leadership: leadership for quality, principal centered leadership, visionary leadership, and the list goes on. Theories, techniques, and management practices constantly evolve, but none are useful or effective if there is no one to step up and take charge. In some areas, the lack of leadership has reached crisis proportions.

Perhaps one of the best (or worst) examples of this leadership crisis is that which exists within the federal government of the United States. Not too long ago the *New York Times* carried an article that quoted an unnamed bureaucrat who said:

> The unequivocal message throughout the federal bureaucracy is that nothing is to be accomplished by this government except the creation of good feelings and the illusion of action...The best and the brightest at my agency and others dutifully exercise caution in substantive matters, avoid action, and continually seek another clearance, another authorization, until someone just finally says no...Matters afflicting the current and future well-being of Americans are seen as mettlesome disruptions that must be calmed, rather than problems that must be solved or responsibilities that must be faced.

The Key to Leadership and Change

Does this revelation surprise anyone? No. Many state and local governments suffer from this same lack of leadership. And the problem doesn't stop there-it exists in the businesses and corporate world as well as public and private institutions. The colleges, universities, and schools within which we work are not immune from this lack of leadership either. Let's hope that it doesn't describe an attitude that exists within your own organization.

The world and conditions around us constantly change. Advances in technology and social issues create conditions that are increasingly complex and uncertain. In today's world, being a good leader is more difficult and demanding than ever before. Facilities managers must take the necessary steps to critique and revitalize their organizations and work diligently to energize, inspire, and empower employees, or your organizations will be much less than they might otherwise be. The old saying applies that if you are not moving ahead, you are falling behind—there is no standing still.

We need to learn this one lesson: the facilities profession lacks more for good leaders than for good managers. Managers are people who get things done by setting goals and objectives, making plans, developing strategies, deciding priorities, obtaining resources, managing people, solving problems, and correcting errors. On the other hand, leaders are the ones who take charge, make things happen, inspire trust, are innovative and original, translate vision into reality, and have a long-range perspective. While managers are needed to get the job done today, leaders are needed to do the job tomorrow.

While most facilities managers work long and hard

at being good managers, the challenge to your profession is to become good leaders as well.

Diversity in the Workforce

The workforce within educational facilities management is ever changing. Not too many years ago the workforce was predominately white males, except for a few female custodians, secretaries, and clerks. The change in the makeup of today's workforce has introduced women and minorities into all areas including custodial, grounds, trades shops, and administration.

Demographics indicate that by the early part of the twenty-first century workers of African-American, Hispanic, Native American, or Asian American decent will outnumber white Americans. Females, likewise, are making up a larger percent of the overall workforce. These changes are having an impact on the workplace, and they create new challenges. Many facilities management organizations are aware of these challenges and have accepted the commitment to move in the direction of having a workforce that is proportional to that which exists in the workforce in their area.

Much has been written and presented about diversity in today's workforce. Understanding and valuing diversity is a skill we must learn if we are to be successful. Valuing diversity and differences means mutual respect, acceptance of others, and a desire to work toward common goals. We must learn to be reciprocal in our accommodations of each other. This means that changes need to take place within the majority culture and sex.

Why should race or sex make a difference in our workforce? As a workforce of growing diversity, you will become an organization that brings together people of various ethnic backgrounds and different sexes in close proximity. What is important to keep in mind is that racism and sexism persist and remain a primary basis for categorizing you and others within society. People often confuse the concepts of culture, which is one's acquired way of life, and race or sex, which are genetically determined. It may be helpful to remember that more than 90 percent of our genetic makeup is identical to that of all humans, only 3 percent determines sexual attributes, and only 2 percent determines our racial characteristics. The remainder shapes individual characteristics.

It is significant that the terms race and racism are often confused. Many people, particularly whites who have had little contact with non-whites, fear that simply recognizing a person's race is being racist. White workers sometimes feel tense and fearful of being prejudiced, while minorities often feel frustrated and impatient with whites who appear prejudiced, or at best naïve. Everyone needs to realize that it is natural and honest to recognize a person's race.

The same thing applies to gender. Males and

females become frustrated with one another because they see the inherent differences between them as indicating value differences rather than just physical differences. Recognition of physical differences is racist or sexist if, and only if, we change our expectations, accept stereotypes, or discriminate or harass on the basis of what we see.

It is incumbent upon us as individuals to accept the changes taking place in today's workforce and to earnestly strive for mutual respect and a willingness to work together for the common good. Those who cannot commit to these requirements have no place within the facilities management profession.

Communication is the Key

Continuous Improvement and Resistance to Change

How do you feel about change? As a general rule, only about 20 percent of the general population is "change-friendly." They are the individuals who are willing to embrace change and perhaps even be an advocate for change. Another 50 percent of the folks are "fence sitters." They assume a neutral position, trying to figure out which way to lean. These people are not hostile to change, but are not willing, without considerable prompting, to make change happen. The other 30 percent are the "resisters." They do not like change and will be antagonistic toward change, and they often make deliberate attempts to thwart change.

Assuming that employees within your organization follow typical norms, the same percentages will exist. Some will embrace change, others will resist change, and the majority will adopt a wait-and-see attitude.

Continuous improvement implies change. If there is a desire to improve a process, alter an attitude, or enhance an end product, some form of change must take place.

Because we live and function within a rapidly changing world, change is inevitable. Technological improvements demand change. Technology is advancing so fast that change occurs in the way things are done at a staggering and ever-increasing pace. As the world is changing, changes are taking place within your institution. And changes are taking place within your facilities management organization too.

Rather than dwell on the concept of change, perhaps it is more productive (and less threatening) to think in terms of improvement. In today's fast-paced world, the most successful organizations—including those that manage facilities—are committed to those functions that are basic to the organization, but also recognize that they too must change or their methods, processes, and products will become obsolete. Therefore, continual improvement becomes the guarantee of survival and success.

Organizations that are successful focus on excellence and quality. They recognize that their products and services must be of superior quality, deliver good value, and improve every time.

When an organization correctly implements quality improvement programs, everyone wins. The customer is happy with the product or service, employees take pride in and feel better about their jobs, and management is motivated to implement further improvements, rather than just putting out fires.

So if everyone wins, why aren't all organizations involved in programs and initiatives that lead to improvement, excellence, and quality? It seems to me there are at least four reasons why some organizations have not joined the continuous improvement movement.

1. Unaware of benefits. Some organizations do not seem to understand the benefits received from implementing such programs and initiatives. If things are going pretty well, you may not be looking for additional improvement. The old saying, "If it ain't broke, don't fix it," seems to be the company motto. These organizations are comfortable in their complacency.

2. Improvement requires change. Many times, management is not willing to challenge the status quo. They let the resisters and fence sitters (who are the majority) reign over the change friendly minority. The barrier to change seems to be impenetrable. The battle cry "we have always done it this way" carries the day.

3. Lack of concern. There are organizations that know all about quality, excellence, and continuous improvement, but they just don't care. They are convinced that no one else really cares whether or not changes are made. And even if they did change, would anyone notice?

4. Too busy putting out fires. Some organizations are so focused on solving daily problems and dealing with emergencies that no time is left to consider alternatives. Their crisis mode of management demands so much attention that there is never any time left to analyze the cause.

Organizations that resist change (for whatever the reason) may not survive. As their methods and services become outdated, outmoded, obsolete, and antiquated, they are likely candidates for extinction, much like the dinosaur. Some will surely fall by the wayside and be replaced by firms and organizations that are proactive in delivering quality products and services.

Is the situation hopeless for those organizations that have yet to see the light, and be converted to receive the salvation offered by continuous improvement? Not really. There are still steps that can be taken to improve quality. Typically, organizations must walk before they run. An old proverb says, "A journey of a thousand miles must begin with a single step." There are several recognized measures that may be followed in order to improve quality within the organization.

Decide to improve. This is perhaps the most important step because it is the first one. Seize the opportunity to pursue quality and don't procrastinate. Do it today.

Measure your success. It is extremely difficult to improve something you can't measure. If you want to improve your customer satisfaction level, you must first know your current level of customer satisfaction. If you want to improve your work order system, you must know what elements are creating the problem and how changes can be monitored.

Get comfortable with change. Understand the people-problems associated with change. People resist change (even the change-friendly types) when they don't understand the need for change or fear they will lose something of value. It is important, therefore, to involve those affected by change in any new program.

Keep raising the bar. Obviously, continuous

improvement is not a one-time effort. No matter how successful you are today, you will secure your future only by continuing to raise your standards.

Keep learning about quality improvement. Study successful organizations and benchmark with your peer institutions. Find out what works and what does not. Attend workshops, seminars, and quality improvement programs. Read APPA's *Strategic Assessment Model,* for example, and network with your peers. Ask questions and keep an open mind. The more you know, the more effectively you can compete.

If you are interested in making change, your job is to justify the struggle and to aim your people toward something special. Plato said, "Those having torches will pass them to others." It's your role to carry the fire and pass the torch. Your survival and that of your organization may depend on it.

The Key to Leadership and Change

Change is Necessary for Progress

As I reflect back over the many years spent working with facilities management organizations, the changes I have seen have been significant. New policies have come and gone. New organizations have done the same. People have come and gone, many have retired.

Everyone is affected by changes taking place around them. In your personal lives there may have been new jobs, moves to different areas, new homes, added family members, new friends, and so forth. How someone handles changes in their life has a direct bearing on how they live. The routine changes that take place on a day-to-day basis are taken in stride. These are usually small and insignificant. But a small change to one person may be a large change to another.

For example, if I was to ask all supervisors to fill out a new form on every employee under their direction and the form would only take a couple minutes to fill out, would it be a big deal? For the lock shop supervisor with only five employees, it isn't a big deal, but for the custodial supervisor with 230 employees, it would be. Luckily, most things you do at work, as well as in your private lives, do not change much on a daily basis. But when small changes add up over time, the differences become immense. Change is inevitable; it's a matter of the attitude you take that determines your reaction to it.

Small changes alter your attitude a little at a time. A few years ago, a friend of mine took a business associate from out of state on a tour of Kennicott Copper's large open pit copper mine located on the west side of the Salt Lake Valley. Eighty-five years ago, a large mountain that consisted of approximately four billion tons of materials stood there. This businessman commented to my friend, "This just proves that we can move mountains, but it requires time, energy, and perseverance."

Most people accept small changes because they don't take much time out of their lives to do so. It only takes a small amount of energy to make the change, and it requires little to put up with the differences it creates.

When big changes come, many don't want to spend the necessary time to understand them; nor do they want to expend the energy to change their pattern of life to adapt to it. The thing people like least of all is persevering through it.

Change comes to all individuals, all organizations, and all institutions. If the attitude towards change is positive, the experiences will normally be positive and worth the effort. If the attitude is negative, then there will be no experience worth using. Our efforts will be wasted, and in the end, each individual involved is a loser.

The Key to Leadership and Change

Whether the changes are large or small, take them a little at a time. Use your energy wisely and persevere to the end. That is progress.

Technology Demands Change

In his book, *New Work Habits for a Radically Changing World*, author Price Pritchett highlights some facts about the rapidly changing world in which we live. For instance, did you know that during the early 1900s, 85 percent of workers were in agriculture; now agriculture involves less than 3 percent of the workforce.

In 1950, 73 percent of U.S. employees worked in production or manufacturing; now less than 15 percent do.

There has been more information produced in the last 30 years than during the previous 5,000 years.

It is no wonder that many of us suffer from an information overload. It is obvious from the statistics that the Industrial Age has given way to the Information Age. The rapid development and acceptance of computers and other electronic devices has been the principal factor in bringing about this transformation.

It is interesting to recall that the first modern computer built in 1944 took up more space than an 18-wheel tractor-trailer, weighed more than 17 mid-sized automobiles, and consumed 140,000 watts of power. This computer could execute up to 5,000 basic arithmetic operations per second. It was a great step forward for its time even though it was quite bulky and expensive. I suspect it was at this point in the development of computers that T. J. Watson, former chairman if IBM, made one of the worst predictions ever when he forecast, "I think there is a world market for about five computers."

By comparison to the size, weight, and capacity of early computers, one of today's popular microprocessors is built around a tiny piece of silicon about the size of a dime, it weighs less than a packet of artificial sweetener, and uses less than 2 watts of electrical power. This computer can execute up to 54 million instructions per second. Its performance seems to improve even before we get our new computer out of the box and operating. Microcomputers are not only a necessity for business operations, but the home market is growing by leaps and bounds as well. Another prediction faux pas was made by Ken Olsen, former president of DEC, who said, "There is no reason for any individual to have a computer in their home."

To link the microcomputer's capability to a familiar example, let's assume you're going to a birthday party and you purchase one of those new-fangled cards that plays the happy birthday jingle when the card is opened. You might be surprised to know that this simple and relatively inexpensive greeting card contains more computer power than existed in the entire world before 1950. The home video camera you'd use to document and record the birthday party contains more processing power than an old IBM 360, the wonder machine that gave birth to the mainframe computer age! And, if the birthday present you give is a popular interactive electronic gaming system, it runs on a processor that has a higher-performance than the original 1976 Cray supercomputer, which in its day was accessible to only the most elite research scientists.

These advances in technology have become so commonplace that today's average consumers wear more computing power on their wrists than existed in the entire world before 1961. So what does all this mean to us who work in the field of facilities management?

One obvious conclusion is that you won't ever again be able to operate in the old way, even if for some irrational reason you desperately want to do so. All jobs will change in some way (many already have) and you will have to perform tasks in a different manner (many already are). And it's not just facilities managers who will be affected by the change. The jobs of your staff will change as well, and they will have to work in significantly different ways.

Changes that take place in how you do your job have not come about because of any wrongdoing on your part. Yet, facilities management organizations and their employees will be held responsible if they don't make change in order to adapt to the "new way." It does little good to try to avoid change, to complain, or be bitter about what's happening.

In fact, such behavior can only do you harm. You will waste precious energy or give in to grief. You jeopardize your future, clinging to old assumptions, old practices, and old expectations about how your job should be done or how the facilities management organization should function. These needed changes may well be more difficult for many of our employees to accept than for those at the mangement level.

As Pritchett says, "Frankly, the world doesn't care about our opinions. Or our feelings. The world rewards only those of us who catch on to what's happening, who invest our energy in finding and seizing the opportunities brought about by change." For your own purposes, you might as well substitute the word "world" in this quote for such words as "institution's administration" or "governing board" or even "boss."

Your success on the job will be measured in how well you meet the challenge of technology and use it to your advantage. To paraphrase a modern saying that seems to apply: Change happens!

Communication is the Key

Managing the Campus of the Future

To create, promote, preserve, disseminate, and apply knowledge is the mission of every college and university. Yet, as we approach the next century, there is reason to reflect on the way that these roles will be fulfilled in the future.

As we continue to move into a new century, we will be required to develop new ways of doing old tasks and we will take on new and different activities. As our institutions move to create an energy that will propel the institution forward to accommodate growth, changes in technology, and changes in the way that basic programs are offered, the facilities managers will be challenged in ways never before imagined.

There are typically two types of facilities managers: the caretaker and the change agent. While both perform necessary tasks, the majority of caretaking functions can be outsourced, while the change agent functions represent value-added facilities management.

We can be assured of one constant as we move into

the next century—change. Everything is going to change and we might as well get used to it. You can take the fatalistic approach or you can be a proactive change agent and initiate change by improving processes, procedures, customer expectations, and employee requirements.

So what do we have to do to accommodate these changes? We have to think cooperation, teamwork, partnerships, and people. We have to think about quality and service, and about our customers. We need to stay updated and in touch. We should seek and welcome an open dialogue about change. Our customers and employees have needs, and we must meet them. We have to prevent damage and excessive deferred maintenance to our facilities, and provide safe and healthful work places. Most of all, we have to provide quality service at a competitive price.

Peterson's Prognostications

I have wet my finger, tested the winds of change, and now make the following prognostications of some of the many anticipated changes that will happen or will continue into the next century:

- Changes will affect the manager and the managed, and emphasize teamwork and partnerships; the focus will be on the bottom line and meeting customer needs.

- Computers will continue to increase in storage capacity and speed.

- Emerging microwave and satellite technology will

develop wireless hand-held computers with the same power as the desktop and laptops of today, and will increase the speed of data transmission and lessen the need for cabling and wiring.

- Basic Internet services will be considered a utility like telephone service, and just as indispensable.

- The next generation will dramatically increase the speed of university and laboratory Internet connections and promote experimentation with new networking technologies.

- Old technologies will be replaced with processes that are better, easier, and more efficient.

- Products and equipment will be more reliable with fewer breakdowns and less maintenance.

- More functions will become voice-operated such as computers, door openers, and parking gates.

- More emphasis will be placed on protecting the worker by maintaining a healthy environment and using personal protective gear and products.

- The number of permanent employees will decrease as temporaries increase.

- Staff will be certified in specific areas of expertise.

- Indoor air quality will become as important as out door air quality and monitoring of indoors environ mental quality will likely take place.

- Changes will be made in the way work is done to reduce the repetitive stresses that lead to carpal tun nel syndrome, bursitis, and other injuries.

- Tools, equipment, and workstations will be redesigned so that they are more ergonomic.

Meeting the Challenges and Changes

What does tomorrow, next year, or the next century hold for your institution, your facilities department, your career, and your ability to provide a value-added function to your organization? The acceleration of change, particularly economic and technological change, is forcing the private sector to review the value of their various holdings, entities, and operations.

The same thing will happen, no doubt, within education. Activities not considered part of the core mission will be candidates for elimination or outsourcing. Facilities managers will be challenged as never before to show how their organization adds value to the institution.

The bright spot in all of this is that the need for building and systems operation and maintenance will never go away. The demands on our profession, our experience, and our expertise can only increase. And that's another thing that's not going to change. I am confident that as a profession, facilities managers will be up to the challenges and changes that are before them.

Section V

Humor: The Key to Survival

A Message to the Downtrodden

After reading one of my last articles, my wife commented that I have become more frivolous in my old age. I suppose she is right, as usual. Not that there is anything wrong with frivolity, but being the astute husband that I am, I believe my wife was making a valid readership comment. I shall attempt to do a more serious piece.

In recent years, great strides have been made in protecting the rights of minorities and females in the workplace. Legislation mandates that facilities and job opportunities must be adapted to accommodate persons with disabilities. The rights of homosexuals are being nationally recognized.

Yet, there is another minority group that continues to be oppressed and made to feel different. This minority group constitutes about 10 to 14 percent of the population, but their cause has never been seriously addressed. These individuals, as they go about their normal activities, are discriminated against numerous times each day. This tormented group of whom I write are those individuals who were born left-handed.

    Left-handed people are different; they have limitations. They cannot use a can opener or most scissors that were obviously designed with the majority in mind. They are incapable of returning a phone to the cradle like "normal" people; it is always backwards. Some of them can't get out of a room because they turn the handle the wrong way. Other barriers are dangerous. The cords on most irons or the moving parts on circular saws and other machinery are menacing invitations to injury for southpaws.

    In the old days, parents and teachers tied left hands behind those inclined to use them. Today, the lives of left-handers are turned into an inside-out obstacle course that is timed by clocks that run from right to left. Lefties arise each morning and struggle into clothing that buttons or zips the wrong way. They risk scalding themselves by using shower handles that turn clockwise. They drive to work in automobiles that have gear shift levers, switches, and dials that must be operated with the right hand.

    At work, they are forced to drink from mugs with the rude and/or cute sayings facing away from them. They work at computer keyboards, typewriters, and adding machines made for right-handers. At lunch, lefties try to find a spot at the table where they are not forced to bump elbows with their seatmates. And so, the day passes with other examples of discrimination and humiliation too numerous to mention.

    The dictionary adds insult to injury by defining left-handed as "clumsy, awkward, backhanded, dubious." Consider, if you will, commonly used phrases that can be offensive to left-handed people: Bill of Rights; right-hand man; right-mindedness; right-of-way; right angle; righteous; right on; right-to-life; right-to-work; and rightist.

It is distasteful for a left-hander to contemplate such phrases as leftovers, left-handed monkey wrench, two left feet, and a left-handed compliment.

There may even be no justice in the next life. The Good Books—the Bible, the Torah, the Koran—lump the worthless and the undesirables on the left side. Those on God's left hand don't even get a hearing on Judgment Day, according to Matthew, Chapter 25: "then shall he say also unto them on the left hand, depart from me, ye cursed, into everlasting fire, prepared for the devil and his angels." Lefties will never get to sit at the right hand of God; they would probably bump elbows. Most folks have the promise of a better life in the eternities, but not lefties. It's downright depressing.

Left-handers need to challenge some basic human assumptions. Why should the left hand have to know what the right is doing? Why should they have to raise their right hand to take an oath? Why do they have to know right from wrong? If they lived south of the equator, where things go their way, maybe things would be different.

It's a Crying Shame

I would venture to guess that left-handers are one of the last surviving minorities in our society with no organization, no collective power or goals, and no real sense of common identity. A sad plight indeed!

I am, let me admit it, a confirmed left-hander. It is nothing I really planned; it just worked out that way, in spite of everything. My parents told me I acquired the habit at a very young age and it has persisted throughout my life.

Allow me to share one of my own personal experiences of discrimination that happened many years ago. I still remember the event as vividly as if it had happened yesterday.

I was just starting first grade in a small two-room country school in Idaho; my teacher was the sister of a local sheriff. It was the first day of school and I recall that I was quite excited to be embarking on an educational journey. Picture in your mind this piquant scene. My left had clutched a newly sharpened pencil, the teacher bending

Communication is the Key

over me as I mark my paper. Firmly she takes the pencil from my left hand and puts it in my right, smiling encouragement. Just as firmly, I return the pencil to my left hand and go on writing. She pries if from my fingers, not smiling now, puts it back in my right hand and shows me her ruler.

Not quite believing and just being a naive first-grader, I switch again. This time I hold on very tightly. It takes both hands to tear the pencil loose. Now, as I watch with an interest that is not unfriendly, she tightly squeezes the fingers of my left hand together in hers, pins my hand flat against the desk, and—I can still feel the pain and surprise—raps my knuckles with the ruler.

Fighting back tears of humiliation and the urge to jab her ample posterior with the point of my sharpened pencil, I realize that my left was too numb to even hold the pencil. Picking up the pencil in my right hand, I submissively attempt to produce a semi-legible scribble on the paper. The attempt is utter failure!

This was the first of many incidents involving corporal punishment at the hands (no pun intended) of my teacher—not all of which I must confess were undeserved. While no visible marks were left on my exterior, alas I fear I was mentally scarred for life.

While I may be stubborn, I am not stupid, which may come as a surprise to all who know me well. After my first incident of discrimination with the pencil, I quickly learned that art of survival by deception. As a practicing and confirmed left-hander, I simply and silently went underground. I would start all writing exercise with my pencil clutched in the right hand. When the teacher would turn her back, the pencil was quickly transferred to the left hand and I would scribble like crazy. My poor penmanship can be attributed to the fact of always having to write fast while keeping one eye on the teacher and the other eye on my work. It raised hob with my eye muscles too.

I did discover at an early age that right-handers draw figures facing left, while left-handers do just the opposite. I was once mortified, and my classmates were sent into fits of giggles, to discover that I had lost my sense of direction and had rendered the udder of an artfully crafted cow under the front legs instead of the back. Being a farm boy I certainly knew better.

In time, even that sort of lateral confusion passed. Cutting figures out of construction paper, however, remained forever beyond me. So do all scissors to this day, requiring as they do, mastery of one among the countless workaday implements engineered, until recently, only for the right-handed majority: handles, screws, gearshifts, rulers (ouch), phone booths, gravy boats, power saws, can openers, corkscrews, violins, guitars, fishing reels, egg beaters, bowling balls, soup ladles, pencil sharpeners, saxophones, potato peelers, and banjos, to name a few.

In closing this treatise on discrimination I submit a few poignant words penned by a kindred spirit and fellow left-hander Benjamin Franklin:

> There are twin sisters of us; and the eyes of man do not more resemble, nor are capable of being on better terms with each other than my sister and myself, were it not for the partiality of our parents, who made the most injurious distinction

between us.

    From my infancy I have been led to consider my sister as a being of a more educated rank. I was suffered to grow up without the least instruction, while nothing was spared in her education. She had masters to teach her writing, drawing, music, and other accomplishments, but if by chance I touched a pencil, a pen or a needle I was bitterly rebuked; and more than once I have been beaten for being awkward and wanting a graceful manner....

So when you chance to meet a left-hander, give them sympathy and try to understand their plight and silent suffering. Do what you can to ease their burdens. A free meal here or a round of drinks there would certainly be appropriate. After all, left-handers are people too.

Humor: The Key to Survival

How to Get a Raise!

By now each of you know whether or not you received an increase in salary for the current fiscal year. Given the propensity of legislators and governing boards to be somewhat tight, if not downright stingy, when it comes to providing money for raises, I would guess that you need all the help you can get in knowing how to get the raise for yourself. After all, you deserve it, right?

Since there is an art to the method of going after a raise, to be successful it must be done properly. The best way seems to fall somewhere between demanding the raise and groveling for it.

About the time you start to hear the rumors about how much money the institution will have available for raises, you should have already started to think through your action plan, if you want to receive your fair share of the pie, or even more. Where do you start? What approach should you take? Do you:

· Start preparing your case by writing down a list of

Communication is the Key

all the good things you do for the institution?

- Slink in on bended knee?

- Send the boss a picture of the new mouth you have to feed?

- Threaten to leave if you don't get the highest raise possible?

I must warn you that there is a major precursor involved with getting a raise. To proceed without considering this vital factor will, in most cases, lead to failure. The key is to have done good work. Radical thought! But let's face it, if you are not doing good work the request for a raise could well be a preliminary exit interview. Experts all agree that the keys to getting a good raise are hard work, good public relations, and a little selling of *you*.

You need to set the stage well ahead of time. Don't just waltz into your boss's office and bluntly ask for the raise, because you will probably get turned down. Nailing a good raise takes a yearlong public relations effort.

Every time you do something exciting, make it visible to your boss. Make sure you inform, but don't overwhelm. For instance, a handwritten note, a brief typewritten memo, or an e-mail message serve the purpose better than a framed 8x10 glossy photo of you shaking hands with the department's employee of the month. Of course, if shaking the hand of the employee of the month was the most exciting thing you did all year, perhaps it would be best to reevaluate your request for a rise.

Be cautious in how you proceed with the actual request. Here are some techniques that could backfire when you ask for a raise:

- **Being too blunt.** Blurting out: "I'd like to talk to you about a raise" might be too direct for some bosses. Remember you want to get a raise, not a rise.

- **Discussing personal problems.** To bring up such personal needs as overwhelming car payments, the expecting of twins, the purchase of a new RV, or rising gambling debts will not help your case. The fact that you have a personal life usually has nothing to do with most bosses or the institution you work for.

- **Being too humble.** A sure kiss of death to a raise request are the words, "I may not deserve it, but…"

- **Begging.** If you go in with your head hanging down, you are begging. If you exhibit a pleading demeanor, you are begging. If you drop to your knees and throw your arms around the boss's legs while beseeching him or her with the words "please, please," you are begging.

- **Talking about other employees.** To say, "George got a raise, why didn't I?" won't win you any points, let alone money.

- **Relying too heavily upon longevity.** Years of loyal dedicated service to the institution may not cut it if the boss knows of a one-year employee who is working circles around you.

- **Making demands.** Avoid saying "I have to have it" or "You owe it to me." If you are demanding, be prepared for the consequences, which usually take one of the following forms: no, hell no, or you're out of here.

The problem most people have in securing a good raise can best be understood in metaphorical terms. Consider this. Most people like to sit by the fire and say, "give me heat," but they don't give any wood. If you give first, the rewards will come later. And if that doesn't work, you'd better dust off the old resume.

Humor: The Key to Survival

Getting No Respect

Sometimes as a facilities manager I feel like the comic Rodney Dangerfield when he says, "Hey, I don't get no respect."

Around the office I was referred to as "The Great Hooey," "The Big Kahuna" or "El Hefa Maximo." At least these are the printable names. One of my supervisors even went so far as to request a formal training session for his workforce on "Respecting Your Supervisor." The justification: "You wouldn't believe what they do to me." Well, join the club. I even had the experience of having my administrative assistant boot me out of my office desk chair, take over my computer, and then tell me to "shut up" when I whined about the takeover. Am I the only facilities manager that gets no respect? I don't think so.

And this was just in my personal relationships within the department. When one moves outside the department things get worse. The dean has no patience with the fact that her office cannot be painted for six months because of the backlog of painting requests caused by downsizing.

Communication is the Key

Another administrator forgets that budget cuts reduced the moving crew by 50 percent and threatens to call the president's office because three rooms of furniture cannot be relocated by noon tomorrow. The budget office maintains that the expensive chiller repairs in Old Main should be funded from the regular maintenance budget and not from the emergency account. And the list goes on and on. Do these people who are caught up in their own self-importance think I would lie to them?

Whatever happened to the time-honored practice of "kissing up" to the boss? Or smiling? Or doing something extra as a favor? Even using the term "yes sir" instead of "hey dude?"

And then there are the mind games that employees play on the boss. Facilities managers are particularly susceptible to mind games since after a few years in the business there just isn't much mind left. Some of the favorite ones used in my organization include: I gave you the report yesterday. You never gave it to me. It's on your desk (a nightmare to a cluttered-desk person). You told me it was due next week. I didn't think you were serious about needing it. I can't get to it now, how about next week?

Talk about no respect. And if that wasn't bad enough, my own boss does it to me too. His favorite missives include: I need this by noon today. Please review this report and tell me what I need to know. You don't have anything special planned for tonight, do you? Let's meet at a convenient location, how about my office? Can you make 20 copies of the report before our meeting in half an hour?

Now, I realize it may seem like an unorthodox approach to most workers, but there are things that can be done on the job to keep the boss happy. And while it may not sit very high on the list of priorities of some workers, there is merit in striving to meet the demands of the boss. I have decided to make it mandatory reading for all employees, those fundamental principles outlined in the document, "Fourteen Steps To Keep Any Boss Happy" which happens to be one of the subtitles of a book titled *Smart Moves*. Surely they will be able to glean something from this assigned reading, which will make it a better place to work, at least for the boss.

And if that doesn't do the job, I suppose I can implement a similar strategy sometimes used to improve morale. You know the technique: "The beatings will continue until morale improves." Who knows, maybe it will work.

After reading this essay, my administrative assistant said with a smile, "Dream on, boss." And then she asked if she should schedule a session with a therapist. I still don't know if she wanted to schedule the appointment for me or for her. Gee, it's tough getting some respect around here.

Bad Attitudes

I don't know about you, but I spend a fair amount of time in my organization trying to instill proper attitudes within my employees, but I have finally realized that I may have a bad attitude myself. In fact, I really hate to bring it up, but a lot of other members of the general public have a bad attitude too. That probably includes most of you.

A friend of mine that I choose to call Frank told me the following story. Frank is a mild-mannered facilities manager who has never been in any kind of trouble—at least nothing serious. One evening as Frank was driving home from work on an unnamed eastern thruway, he came to a toll plaza. He pulled up to the booth and held out his $1.25. At this point, the toll-taker pulled out a very large pile of $1.00 bills and started to count them very slowly. Cars began to pile up behind Frank, some started to honk. Then more people were honking, shouting, gesturing, possibly rummaging through their glove compartments in search of firearms. And the slow counting countinued.

Humor: The Key to Survival

In desperation, Frank, despite being mild-mannered, did a bad thing. In fact he did three bad things: 1) he made an explicit, non toll-related suggestion to the toll-taker; 2) he threw his $1.25 into the booth; and 3) he drove away.

He didn't get very far, of course. Western civilization did not get to where it is today by tolerating this kind of flagrant disregard for toll procedures. Frank was swiftly apprehended, taken to the police station, and narrowly missed being sent to prison only by applying a shrewd legal maneuver of paying the $50 fine.

So justice was done, but this story illustrates my point about the bad public attitude. Too many of us are, like Frank, guilty of assuming that everything is set up for our benefit and convenience. When we pull up to a toll booth we expect to just hand the attendant the money without realizing that this person might have other things to do, and that it might be more convenient for him or her if we came back another time.

I also get weary of hearing complaints about postal clerks. Just because a person works for the postal service does not mean this person has nothing better to do than help you conduct postal transactions. Recently, while waiting in line at a post office to purchase stamps, I was shocked to hear people muttering because the three clerks behind the counter were moving so slowly. To the untrained eye, the clerks did not appear to be waiting on anybody. They appeared to be legally dead, although I believe dead people are more animated, due to bacterial action.

I wanted to tell the complainer, "If you don't like standing in line for 45 minutes while three clerks fulfill what is apparently some kind of postal service requirement to display the same energy level as linoleum, take your business to some other postal service." But of course, I didn't say anything because it may have violated a postal regulation and they might have put me in prison, or worse sent me to the end of the line.

The most serious public attitude problem I have encountered was in an Arizona Department of Motor Vehicles facility, where I attempted to renew my driver's license. I heard a lot of ill-mannered grumbling from members of the public, especially the ones who had been there more than three days. Most folks didn't talk very loud because of the prominent sign with three-inch letters indicating that the clerks didn't have to serve you if you were nasty to them.

Again, just because these people had been told that they could renew their licenses at the facility, they expected to just waltz in and—talk about gall—renew their licenses. You can imagine how irritating this was for the Department of Motor Vehicles employees, who already had their hands full with other duties, which include: taking breaks, informing you that you've been standing in the wrong line for the past hour, and taking additional breaks.

I must confess that even I started to develop an attitude problem after a couple of hours. When I got to the counter and the clerk asked if I wanted to be an organ donor, I almost shouted, "No! I want to donate your organs!" Fortunately, I restrained myself.

My point is that members of the public need to stop assuming that the government has nothing better to do than serve them. In addition, you need to straighten out your attitude toward the phone company and hospitals. Hospitals would be a lot more pleasant for people who work in them if you didn't keep coming in with medical problems.

And don't forget about newspapers. They're sick and tired of your telling them that you didn't get your paper. Newspapers have enough trouble printing the paper; they can't worry about whether or not you actually receive it. So just hold your complaints. You're probably in the wrong line anyway.

Communication is the Key

Some People are Like Potatoes

Idaho is world famous for its potatoes. I grew up on a farm in southeastern Idaho, where potatoes were raised as one of the staple crops. Potatoes are very important to the economy of the state. Potatoes are also referred to as spuds, tators, and tubers. I recall that during the annual potato harvest period in the fall, school was dismissed for two weeks as a "harvest vacation" since family members were needed to complete the harvest. To this day, the nearest community to our farm still holds an annual "Spud Day" that celebrates this important commodity.

I am well acquainted with potatoes and recognize that potatoes have been an important part of my life. Currently, the most important part that potatoes play in my life happens at mealtime. I love to eat them. Even with all the memories of the hard work associated with cutting seed, planting, weeding, cultivating, spraying, irrigating, digging, sacking, hauling, storing, and then worrying about the selling price of potatoes, they are still one of my favorite foods.

Humor: The Key to Survival

I have obviously spent a lot of time around potatoes and have come to the conclusion that some people are like potatoes. For example:

SpecTators. There are those who are content to watch while others make plans and carry out the work. They would rather sit on the sidelines and let someone else carry the ball. SpecTators seem to enjoy what they do best (watch), but never experience the satisfaction of making the "big play" themselves. Rarely do SpecTators get recognized or are given much responsibility. As a result, they are rarely successful as productive workers.

CommentTators. Some never help, but are gifted at finding fault and telling others how to do the job. CommentTators never miss an opportunity to tear down the ideas of others and concentrate on discussing why things can't be done a certain way. When all is said and done, as a CommentTator, there is much more said than done.

AgiTator. There are people who cause problems by asking others to agree with them on issues large and small such as it's too hot or too cold, too light or too dark, too wet or too dry. Nothing is ever just right for them and because they seem to be miserable, they want others to agree with their point of view. They originated the phrase, "Misery loves company."

HezzieTators. There are people who say they will help, but somehow they never get around to it. When there is work to do, HezzieTators are found looking the other way. They find it hard to commit, they are slow to react and are loath to take action. They operate as in a fog; like they are lost. In fact, the saying, "He who hesitates is lost," certainly applies to this person.

EmmaTators. There are some people who pretend to be someone they are not. Some EmmaTators would like you to think they are hard workers, but they're not. Others would like you to think they are competent, but they're not. Still others would like you to think they are honest and trustworthy, but they're not. EmmaTators get by for awhile, but the "true" person shows up before long.

DickTators. Those who are bossy and like to tell others what to do or where to go, but would not soil their own hands to get there may be called DickTators. These folks think there is only one way to do things—their way. DickTators don't usually stay in one place for long.

SweetTators. Thank goodness there are those who smile and do what they say they will do. They are always prepared to lend a helping hand. They bring real sunshine into the lives and work of others. They make work and life flow more smoothly for everyone. And they do it with a sincere smile.

What kind of Tator are you?

Humor: The Key to Survival

Needed: A University Garage Sale

On occasion I succumb to the primal inner urge found within a fairly significant portion of the human population to bag a real bargain. In pursuit of that urge I have been known to strike out on a Saturday morning to stalk the garage sale trail. On rare occasions I have even succeeded in procuring that elusive once-in-a-lifetime bargain. On the other hand, periodic necessity has dictated that I sponsor my own personal garage sale in order to free up enough space in the garage to park the family automobile.

As I look around at the crowded facilities within my institution, I have concluded that the university would benefit from having its own garage sale—a university-wide garage sale, if you will. While we recognize that the university has an organized and perfectly legitimate method of disposing of surplus property, that process deals only with items that are openly acknowledged as useless, nonfunctional, or obsolete.

What really concerns me are those forgotten items

that are squirreled away in closets, storage rooms, and other less-than-legal locations, or those items that are kept because someday they will surely be needed (most likely the day after hell freezes over).

Prior to this grandiose garage sale, we might even go so far as to require every faculty member, every administrator, and all staff to evaluate every piece of equipment and all materials that he or she is responsible for. Only those items in good condition or that have been used directly to support the mission of the institution during the past fiscal year would be retained. The remainder of the items would be part of the gigantic university garage sale. I have a good feel for the magnitude of this problem on our campus, but try to visualize, if you will, the space that could be freed up and gained in all our schools if each institution conducted its own garage sale.

The room that has housed broken desks and chairs for the past 20 years would be empty again and available for constructive use, like instruction or research. Those moth-eaten and dusty stuffed critters and the jars of pickled snakes could be transferred to someone's private trophy room or at least given a decent burial. Relics such as adding machines, typewriters, 64k personal computers, and other electronic equipment of a bygone era might be put to beneficial use by bargain-seeking retirees, or donated to a museum. The space gained could be staggering, and who knows what skeletons would be unearthed.

Old and mysterious awards, certificates, plaques, trophies, and other memorabilia would disappear from offices and storage cabinets. Old copies of the *Chronicle of Higher Education*, the *Wall Street Journal*, *American School &*

Humor: The Key to Survival

University magazine, and other journals and periodicals would free up space on bookshelves, storerooms, and more importantly in libraries, which could then be filled with more current periodicals or even computers.

And we should not ignore the teaching and research laboratories. Who knows what antiques would be found? The spaces occupied by discarded beakers, outdated chemicals, and broken test tubes alone could add significant usable storage.

Classroom closets never opened by instructors could be cleaned out and made available to start a new life as usable storage areas. Custodians could remove obsolete and unused cleaning products, broken equipment, and the pile of instructions and policy changes accumulated over the past 30 years.

The maintenance shops could do well to clean house too. Not just cleaning house but removing accumulated pipe scraps, broken equipment, parts, fittings, nails, screws, and bolts that combine in weight to wreak havoc on the overloaded springs of each service vehicle. Shop storage could be greatly increased if those obsolete and never-to-be-used-again products were disposed of. Someone with appropriate authority could remove those items illegally stored under stairways, in corridors, hallways, and equipment rooms. Especially equipment rooms.

Assuming that every building was originally planned and built to include adequate storage (a questionable assumption indeed), the storage spaces would likely have been completely filled within the first year of building occupancy. The storage scenario usually goes like this: file cabinets fill up very fast, then portable storage units are brought in to accommodate a few more months of storage needs, and then arrives boxes of all sizes that are stored in every location imaginable and even some unimagined locations.

I do, however, have a major reservation about this garage sale. My concern: who will attend? My greatest fear is that our own faculty and staff will purchase most of the items and the whole operation will merely result in the removal of items from one storage location to someone else's stock of useless items. There must be a way to do it right.

I have a selfish reason for sharing this idea with you. After working as a facilities manager for nearly 30 years, I would just once like to hear, when I ask a dean or department head about their most serious space need, something like, "I don't have any space needs-especially for storage." I recognize that I am dreaming to think a conversation such this would ever take place.

Of course, I have other dreams as well, like having an adequate budget sufficient to reduce deferred maintenance levels and to pay for unfunded mandates. I am cynical of the possibility that these funds will be forthcoming through normal funding channels, however, and have concluded that I may have a better chance if I make friends with Bill Gates.

Humor: The Key to Survival

How to Beat the Meeting Trap

Have you ever walked out of a meeting thinking, "What a total waste of time!" or "For this I got a college education?"

Seemingly, there are two things that no college or university can live without. Institutions of higher education have learned to survive budget cuts, losing football teams, tenured faculty, and administrative scandals, but they would be dead-in-the-water without: 1) committees, and 2) meetings. These two ever-present features of academe will always be with us. I'm working on how to beat the meeting trap. How to deal with committees still eludes me. It has occurred to me, however, that most committees function by holding meetings. I may be making progress.

When it comes to meetings, the first thing you need to realize is that you are not a meeting attendee—you are a meeting victim. It may be sort of like suddenly realizing you are not really a party dude, you just have an alcohol problem.

If you are a meeting victim, you probably look forward to meetings with as much anticipation as running a marathon race with an ingrown toenail. Business gurus will tell you that meetings gobble up to 70 percent of many employees' time. If that's not being victimized, I don't know what is. May I suggest some techniques that may help you beat the meeting system?

Agenda Power. Each person comes to the table with their own agenda, but the person that sets the main agenda is the one that controls the meeting. The secret to influencing the meeting (for those with less power) is to influence the main agenda. When your turn to respond comes around, try to have something more meaningful to say than "pass."

90/10 Rule. Remember that 90 percent of all meeting time is focused on the first 10 percent of the agenda. If you must sleep in the meeting, do so later rather than sooner.

Table Position is Everything. Sit across the table from whoever is running the meeting. If things are going badly for you, there is a good chance you can distract that person by performing some odd facial distortions or some subtle body gestures. The rule here is don't get carried away.

The Use of "We." Always use the term "we" when making a point. Not only will there be emphasis on the group process and your ideas will look like contributions, but everyone else at the table will think that they are the only ones not with you. It is difficult for them to challenge you since they are obviously in the minority.

Non-Verbal Cues. Stay alert for non-verbal cues from participants. If more than half the attendees are looking out the window you know that they have no interest in the subject being discussed. Yawns are also a good indicator. Snoring is a dead giveaway. The sure tip-off of disinterest is the fellow at the far end of the table with an ear-mounted radio speaker attached to the off-side ear farthest from the person in charge. It does no good to emulate these cues yourself, since it usually encourages those in charge to call another meeting.

Be Assertive. Learn to be assertive about your ideas without being obnoxious. Pounding the table with your shoe may have worked for Kruschev, but it may be overkill when meeting with the president's cabinet.

Know When to Shut Up. You don't have to involve yourself in every debate. In fact, if the situation doesn't directly concern you, it may be wise to duck and say nothing. As the old saying goes, "It is better to appear stupid, than to open your mouth and remove all doubt."

Stand Up if Possible. Standing represents a position of authority. Once the commitment is made to stand, however, it is a sign of weakness to sit. Standing may not be a wise strategy for long and drawn out meetings.

Try meeting in a room with no chairs. That way nobody gets comfortable. You can get right to the point. This may be easier said than done. If you ever tried to find a room with no chairs, you realize it is either the hallway or the furnace room. On second thought, I take that back. The maintenance staff had hauled some chairs into the last furnace room I visited. That may leave only the hallways.

Avoid Being Accusatory. Avoid accusatory statements or questions. Instead, start with a positive statement. For example one might say, "I'm really glad you're making a priority for stress reduction within the department. And (never say 'but') I am positive that you are the cause of my personal stress." See the positive statement?

Well, there you have it: some simple rules of survival for meetings. If followed, they may not help you enjoy meetings more, but if executed with skill, persistence, and due diligence, they should result in getting you invited to fewer meetings.

Humor: The Key to Survival

Dodging Bullets, Scythes, and Maces

I've heard it said over the years that tenure in the positions of university presidents and facilities managers are both around seven years. The main difference between the two is that most presidents have the advantage of academic tenure, and as they depart the presidency they gracefully transfer back into the role of distinguished professor. On the other hand, facilities managers usually just hit the streets in a most undistinguished manner.

This seven-year thing seems to be the common denominator in a wide variety of bad happenings. For instance, there were the seven plagues of Egypt orchestrated by Moses, seven year's bad luck, the seven deadly sins, seven year cycle of wet and dry years, and even the seven year itch. I'm sure you get the picture.

When I completed my tenth year of non-tenured service at Arizona State University, I wondered if I was overdue for the good news/bad news thing. You know, the good news: my boss tells me he has arranged for me to have more free time, fewer meetings, and no budget has-

Communication is the Key

sles; and the bad news: I am now unemployed.

Maybe my subconscious thoughts have been working overtime in this area because the other night I had a dream. Well perhaps it was more like a nightmare. In the dream, I had a meeting scheduled with my boss. As I was ushered into his office, I immediately noticed that he was wearing a new outfit. He looked strikingly like the grim reaper. Upon closer inspection, however, I astutely observed that his robe looked more like academic regalia and instead of having a scythe slung across his shoulder, it was a ceremonial mace (the ornamental staff borne by an important academician in the graduation parade).

As a historical note, I should point out that academia has adopted as its ceremonial mace a more refined version of the heavy spiked staff used in the Middle Ages for breaking armor. Even though more refined, kinder, and gentler, a ceremonial mace in the hands of a bad-tempered and determined boss could really do a number on one's vulnerable body parts. That's all I need: to get "maced" out of a job.

The alarm clock went off about this time in the dream, so I don't really know what happened. Since this nocturnal episode may have been a premonition of impending doom, I decided I had better brush up on a few things I might need to know if forced into a job search. Through an exhilarating cruise of the Internet, I found it critically important that the unemployed be up-to-speed on the newer job search jargon so as not to be duped into accepting a position that would be a real bummer.

As a result of this helpful bit of research, I was able to garner the real meaning of some commonly used job search lingo. For instance, here's a little clarification of some terms:

Humor: The Key to Survival

Competitive salary: We remain competitive by paying less than our competitors.

Join our fast-paced company: We have no time to train you and you are on your own. Good luck.

Seeking enthusiastic, fun, hard-working people: All our folks are a bunch of slugs.

Casual work atmosphere: We don't pay enough to expect that you'll dress up; although a couple of the real daring guys wear earrings.

Join our dynamic team: We need another body to jump on the treadmill that runs our dynamo.

Must be deadline oriented: You'll be six months behind schedule on your first day.

Some overtime required: Some time each night, and some time each weekend.

Duties will vary: Anyone in the place can boss you around.

Must have an eye for detail: We have no quality control.

Advanced degree preferred: Unless you wasted those extra years studying something like philosophy or English.

No phone calls please: We've filled the job; our request for resumes is just a legal formality.

Seeking a candidate with a wide variety of experiences: You'll need it to replace the three people who have just left.

Problem-solving skills a must: You're walking into a company in perpetual chaos.

Requires team leadership skills: You'll have the responsibility of a manager without the pay or status.

Communication is the Key

Good communication skills: Management communicates, you read their minds, figure out what they really want, then do it.

Now that I understand the terms, when the ax falls (or more appropriately the mace) I will be much better prepared to hit the streets running. That's assuming the boss misses on the first swing.

By the way, how long did you say you've been in your current position? Better get prepared now so you won't get "maced" out of your job!

Humor: The Key to Survival

The Retirement Report

Everywhere I go folks ask me, "Hey Peterson, how is retirement?" So people won't feel obligated to ask, I'm submitting this report.

Before retirement I would tell people that "work was starting to interfere with my fun." I suppose that was a subtle way of telling them that work was no longer as fun as it used to be. I return to the university just enough to confirm that retirement was the right decision. When one retires there is an assumption that you will have all sorts of extra time to do those things you never had time to do while holding down a full-time job.

I don't know where all the hours go, but I've joined the ranks of retirees who maintain, "I don't know how I ever had time to work." I had heard that part of the daily routine of retirees was to take an afternoon nap. If in fact retirees take naps, I don't know how they do it since I haven't found time for one. I take that back, I did take a short nap last October, but that's it.

Since retirement, my wife has started to give out sub-

Communication is the Key

tle hints that my extra presence around the house is starting to annoy her. You should have seen her fume when I reorganized her spice rack. You would have thought she would appreciate having all those spices arranged in alphabetical order. It certainly made more sense to me than the completely random system that she has used ever since we were married. Evidently, she really likes her random system.

When I started eyeing up the pantry for another organizational project, she booted me clean out of the kitchen. She has now started to make me a daily agenda that for some strange reason schedules me out of the house a lot. No, she doesn't type up a daily shirt-pocket schedule, what my secretary used to call the "idiot card." I have to do it myself. You know I can just hear Robin from the old office hooting over the fact that "the idiot must now make up his own card."

And speaking about work, once you retire things are never the same when you go back to the office. For example, the other day I was invited back for a scheduled event for which my presence had been formally requested, RSVP and the whole bit. I tried all the usual close parking places, but they were either full or I didn't have the right decal. I had to park half a mile away and hike to the event. Now I better understand all those nasty comments about parking on campus. Maybe I'll get a skateboard like the students or better yet one of those newfangled scooters.

One other time when I went to campus (invited of course) they took pity on me and allowed me to park my personal vehicle inside the fenced compound with a promise not to call parking services or the tow truck. But that was only after I couldn't find a parking place and threatened to leave.

I rarely just pop in the plant unannounced or uninvited anymore. I find myself not as welcome as I used to be when I was the boss. Or at least staff used to put on a better act. I feel grateful that the receptionist still acknowledges me and remembers my name. But no one is ever in his or her office when I show up. They must have developed an early warning system since my departure. And so I spend more time calling people on the telephone. The caller ID must be working pretty well too because they never answer the phone. I leave messages on their voice mail, but they never return my calls. Oh well, I guess they aren't interested in any more of my unsolicited advice on how the place ought to be run.

Last year I attended a regional conference for the first time as an APPA emeritus member. It was the only time I ever sluffed all the educational sessions and participated with the partners in their program. My suspicions were confirmed: they do have more fun. I could come up with no logical reason to attend the educational sessions to learn how to do my job better when I no longer have a job. Due to my status as an old geezer, however, I was invited to make a presentation at one of the sessions. Thank goodness it was the final session and they didn't ruin all my fun. The presentation required someone who could remember the "good old days" and there were only two of us who were the designated codgers.

I am somewhat reticent to admit that to get ready for the presentation I was forced to do considerable research about how things used to be. Most certainly I was there, but my memory has a few gaps (more like chasms). The host school did its best to make us feel right at home with an informal setting that included comfortable easy chairs, a coffee table, and cold drinks. Since the other guy's institution hosted the conference I suspect he had some pull in this regard. Folks must have liked our presentation since at its conclusion we received a standing ovation. Or was it that everyone was on their feet headed for the exit doors by the time we wrapped things up. Probably one of the hazards of being scheduled just prior to the social hour.

My wife and I have recently spent a lot of time traveling. A few years back (or so it seems) I used to just jump in the car and head down the road. I could find my way almost anywhere without asking for directions. Besides, asking for directions is my wife's job. In the old days I was so good at finding the way, my wife referred to me as "the pathfinder." You know, like Kit Carson. My sense of direction was guided as if my mind contained a precision compass. Maybe that metal plate in my head now affects the compass.

On the last trip, I got lost twice. And that was before I got out of Phoenix. I now rely on detailed road maps. I joined the American Automobile Association because they have very good maps. Another really helpful service for the directionally challenged is written instructions that put you on the right roads and streets and give distances to each turn or turn off. I suppose I would have reached the right destination using their detailed travel plan, but my eyes aren't what they used to be. I couldn't read the print. Next time I will check to see if they have large print copies for old geezers. Maybe its time to make a visit to the optometrist. Or I could get one of the devices that use satel-

Humor: The Key to Survival

lite technology that talks you through every twist and turn along the way. Nah, it would probably require programming and there are no kids at home anymore.

When we leave the car home and turn the driving over to someone else, we usually fly. Since retirement I have become very savvy about the airlines. I have discovered the secret of how to get peanuts instead of pretzel snacks and how to con the flight attendant out of an entire soft drink rather than settling for one of those pitifully small plastic cups filled to the brim with ice and two ounces of soda pop. Yes, really. I have also found the best seats on the airplane and even how to finagle upgrades to first class seating.

My last experience in first class, however, was a real bummer. You may have read about the lady who conned the airlines into allowing her pet pig to travel with her in the cabin as a "service animal." Evidently the lady gets very depressed when separated from her pig. Well as luck would have it, I was given the seat just across the aisle from the lady and her pig.

No the pig didn't have a seat, but it was given permission to lay in the aisle beside her mistress. Contrary to the pastoral scene painted by the news media, the flight wasn't without incident. The 300-pound porker must have eaten some bad greens in the airport café which caused her to pass voluminous quantities of odoriferous flatulence about every 15 minutes or so. After that stink I will never feel guilty again for my own slight indiscretions in public.

I should have guessed that something bad was happening in the bovine's bowels. When the plane descended for landing, the decreased cabin pressure not only affected the pig's inner ear but also her bowels. She went berserk just prior to landing and raced around the entire first class cabin squealing loudly and filling the galley opposite the plane's exit with a considerable quantity of the byproduct from the greens previously consumed.

Luckily, the plane's ventilation system didn't confine the smell to just the immediate area. It very effectively dispersed the odor throughout the airplane. It was the first time I had ever seen the flight attendants be the first ones up the runway. They had to hurry to beat the pilot and copilot. I made myself quite unpopular with the lady by suggesting she clean up after her porker. She left that to the cleanup crew. Next time she flies I hope she will rely upon depression medication and not the pig.

Since retirement, one of my projects has been to work on eradication of the pesky ants out in my yard. They seem to favor a spot in the front yard next to the sidewalk. Initially, I did the genteel things and applied some insecticide stuff. According to the experts, this product tastes like candy to the ants. The obedient worker carried the stuff deep inside the anthill. If things go in accordance with the manufacturer's instructions, the queen ant is supposed to eat the stuff and croak. The bereaved ant colony is then duty bound to make a pilgrimage to the neighbor's yard, where they hope for better treatment.

My ants must be dumber than those used in the manufacturer's tests, because they merely move along the sidewalk about a foot and start digging again. I've tried bug sprays, water, and fire, but still they persist. I even once resorted to anthill vandalism and dug up one of the ant condos. That only made them mad and I ended up with 27 painful bites. Nothing seems to work. I must admit I spend more time working on my anti-ant project now than when I was gainfully employed. The discouraging thing is that the ant problem has gotten worse since my retirement. How can that be?

Last summer shortly after my retirement and while making an out-of-state family visit, I took my four-year-old grandson on a walk. While on the walk we found lots of interesting sights, sounds, and treasures that excite a young boy. We found a really neat stick just lying on the ground; we collected a whole pocketful of colorful pebbles; we paused to admire horses and cows in a field; we talked to several pet dogs along the way; and we walked around a really large anthill. The anthill made the ones in my own yard look like podunk city. We even collected a wide variety of leafy twigs and flowers. The walk was a delightful experience.

One another trip in November we visited the same family. My grandson remembered the previous walk and insisted we go again. Even though I was miserable with a feverish cold and persistent cough, I agreed. The weather was much colder and I suggested we make an abbreviated trip, but the four-year-old would hear nothing of it. We had to take the exact same route as the previous walk. He had a much more difficult time collecting treasures since his hands were covered with heavy gloves. He instead found more sport in getting wet and dirty by kicking in the snow and walking through the mud.

Evidently the thrill and memory of the previous walk faded quickly because within a short time he complained that his feet hurt. Then it was his butt. When his stomach started to hurt, we headed back toward home. He had no interest in collecting dried twigs and frozen flowers, so I had to do it so he wouldn't be disappointed. He did find a sturdy stick, which he carried home to worry the family dog with. I decided some experiences are better not repeated.

Well, all in all I highly recommend retirement. While I don't seem to have any more time, I am having more fun. I spend time doing those things I want to do rather than doing what someone else (like the boss) wants me to do. I now take time to smell the flowers after I photograph them. I watch the sunsets rather than merely glance at them in passing. I do some serious exercise rather than merely ogling the girls in the gym. And no, it's not that I am too old to ogle.

About the Author

H. Val Peterson recently retired after spending over 33 years as a facilities manager at two major universities, Utah State University and Arizona State University. He is a licensed professional mechanical engineer and spent a portion of his career working as a consulting engineer. Peterson has been a member of the Association of Higher Education Facilities Officers (APPA) and the Rocky Mountain Association of Higher Education Facilities Officers (RMA) since 1970, and has served as President of both organizations, in addition to serving on the Board of Directors and various committees and task forces. He wrote regular feature columns in APPA's *Facilities Manager* magazine and RMA's *Smoke Signals* and *Rocky Mountain Views* newsletters. He lives with his wife in Chandler, Arizona. The author welcomes e-mail at: valpeterson@asu.edu.